Dead As I'll Ever Be

by Pamela Evans

Published by: Crossquarter Publishing Group
Xemplar imprint
PO Box 8756
Santa Fe, NM 87504 USA
(505) 438-9846 voice/fax

Many happy lifetimes ahead.

Warmest regards,

Dead As I'll Ever Be
Copyright © 2002 Pamela Evans
Cover photograph of author by Lisa Bennett

ISBN: 1-890109-37-1 All rights reserved.

All rights reserved. No part of this book may be reproduced without written permission of the publisher, except by a reviewer who may quote brief passages in a review with appropriate credits; nor may any part of this book be reproduced, stored in a retrieval system, or transmitted electronically, without the written permission of the publisher.

Printed in Canada on recycled paper.

Acknowledgements

This book was a team effort.

Thank you—to my husband David, my best friend, who cheerfully survived a crash-course in homemaking and errands over the last few months of the book. To my daughter Lisa, who patiently snapped three rolls of film to get one photo that didn't make me groan. To my son Gray, who insisted I use our computer to write the book, and who would say, "Don't panic, Mom, you haven't lost the whole chapter. Look in the 'Recycle Bin,'" in response to my calls.

To all my family, friends and acquaintances who gave me permission to use their stories—thank you. You've opened the door for others to talk about their own mysterious experiences that often transcend all religious teachings.

To my London editor, Helen MacKenzie, who not only straightened out my punctuation, but also, being unfamiliar with reincarnation and a Virgo (born to notice the flaws), was the perfect test market. And to Anthony Ravenscroft, who shaped this book better than I could have imagined.

To actress and author Shirley MacLaine, for introducing the concept of reincarnation to the general public many years ago with her first metaphysical book, *Out on a Limb,* and for teaching other spiritual topics in her subsequent books. Her fame, intelligence, and courage made the going easier for the rest of us.

And to my unseen helpers—thanks.

Dedication

To Mary Muhlmann,
who started the quest.

Table of Contents

Chapter 1: How It All Started 1

Chapter 2: My Bizarre Spiritual Background
    and Other Events 23

Chapter 3: Marge 49

Chapter 4: Three Favorite Seances 67

Chapter 5: The Seminars 77

Chapter 6: Astrology Explained a Lifelong
    Conflict 101

Chapter 7: Life's Patterns 111

Chapter 8: Palmistry 123

Chapter 9: My Reincarnation Experiences 131

Chapter 10: Teaching About Reincarnation 137

Chapter 11: Ghosts 171

Chapter 12: Stories from Friends
    and Acquaintances 179

Chapter 13: Summing Up 203

Appendix: Suggested Reading 209

About the Author 213

1
How It All Started

Mary

During lunch, Jane talked me into trying a psychic reading. That was twenty years ago, and I haven't been the same since.

We chatted in a half-empty restaurant, the clatter around us dwindling to the odd clang of a dropped fork or bang of a tray being stacked. My gaze slipped past her to the glassed-in front of the restaurant and the gunmetal March sky beyond. As she was talking, my drifting attention was creating a beach scene... *Paul Newman, tenderly anointing my back with lotion, was about to seal his achievement with a kiss...* when Jane interrupted the reverie by saying, "...and then she said I'd meet this man with salt-and-pepper hair, who came from the east... at the home of friends... and it happened!"

She was talking about a psychic she'd just visited. I looked at her. "Tell me again," I said, "I missed some of the first part." She did, with more specific details the psychic had told her. The psychic's name was Mary.

At the time, I knew nothing about psychics. I remembered that one had told a friend of mine when she was in high school that there would be a death in the family within a year. Her father had a sudden heart attack and died within 12 months of the reading. I shivered at the time, but hadn't thought much more about it.

Years later, I heard another friend's story. A psychic had described her husband's girlfriend and given details of the girlfriend's personality. They turned out to be true. That was interesting, but... who knows? The psychic had been reassuring about my friend's future, giving her a glimmer of hope that I dismissed at the time.

Books about haunted houses had always intrigued me, and I loved arguing with anyone about the reality of ghosts. During my 30-year agnostic phase as a "recovering Anglican," I'd wrestled the subject of life-after-death to the ground. Death was final—period.

"Do you want to go?" asked Jane.

"Sure," I said. Why not?

I was reasonably content with my life. I'd more or less accepted the limitations of being a free-lance fashion illustrator and copy writer in London, Ontario (population 300,000) and realized that working out of town, particularly in Toronto (Canada's advertising Mecca), was out for a few years. I played tennis and bridge. Family and friends, reading and work filled my days, so I wasn't going to a psychic as a last resort to solving a problem.

Jane made the appointment from the restaurant, for four o'clock that afternoon. It was 2:30 when she called. (No time for the psychic to do any research.) She didn't mention my last name. An attack of butterflies settled in as she hung up the phone. I certainly wasn't going to take anything the psychic said seriously!

❧ ❧

Driving up the gravel driveway to Mary's small white bungalow, my butterflies changed to anxious shivers. A small homemade sign stood in the middle of the front lawn, reading simply "Mary." We drove around an apple tree and parked behind the house. Another

How It Started

similar sign hung above the back door. Climbing out of the car, I noticed a small graveyard just beyond the neighbor's fence and shivered again. As if that wasn't enough, a black cat joined us at Mary's back door and waited to be let in.

Nothing happened for about a minute after we rang the doorbell. Then we heard footsteps. The door opened and a Walter Matthau look-alike scrutinized us. He wore an old gray cardigan and baggy brown pants. In a funereal voice, he said, "Who are you?"

I didn't like him.

Jane reminded him that she'd been there before, and introduced us. This was Mary's husband, Paul.

"Come in and sit down," he said, "we're in the middle of a reading. Mary will see you presently." We followed him through the glassed-in porch, into a small dark room. The only light came through two tiny high windows. An old sofa and an assortment of kitchen chairs surrounded a kidney-shaped coffee table piled high with the *National Enquirer* and other "neon" publications. Exchanging amused smiles, we sat down, and I lit a cigarette. I couldn't get rid of my feeling of unease.

Paul explained that he sat in on the readings to translate for those who didn't speak German. He told us to make ourselves comfortable, excused himself, closed the door and disappeared into the kitchen. I didn't want him in the room for my reading.

Jane made herself comfortable. The gaudy "literature" might have been entertaining at some other time but I was too nervous to concentrate even on junk. Jane filled me in with other accurate predictions and facts that Mary had told her. Every new piece of information increased my toe tapping until I thought I was going to have to pace the floor. I'm a nervous Nelly at the best of times, not about big events or disasters, but about small things—though *this* small thing turned into one of the biggest events of my life.

Finally, we heard voices approaching and the door from the kitchen opened. Paul and a middle-aged woman came into the room, deep in conversation. The woman seemed like a regular visitor and appeared quite relaxed after her reading. (Maybe it *wasn't scary*.) Saying goodbye, she left.

"Mary will see you now," announced Paul, looking at me.

"*What am I doing here?*" I thought, following him through the door into an ordinary-looking kitchen. Not a broom in sight. We crossed the kitchen to a small room where Mary waited. Paul paused inside the doorway to say something to her in German while I tried to peek around him. Mary, from the side view I caught, was small and round with gray hair skinned back in a small bun. She wore something shapeless and blue. Rocking slightly back and forth, she held one hand to her forehead. She remained turned away from me, with her eyes closed.

Paul pointed to a chair attached to a tiny table in front of Mary. I had to sit sideways and turn my upper body to the left to face her. A gooseneck lamp focused light on a pad of paper resting on a small flat pillow on the table.

"Just sign your name, and write down your birthday and two or three names of anybody else you want Mary to talk about," said Paul, parking himself on the edge of an old green sofa beside us.

Mary's round face was scrunched up with concentration. She looked older than Paul. Intense blue eyes suddenly opened and looked at me. She must have reached some sort of conclusion while her eyes were shut and, having done that, took my hands in hers, turned up my palms, pressed her thumbs to the base of my third finger on both hands and spoke in a stream of German.

I waited.

"She says you have talents untried," translated Paul, "talents in the public eye... television... radio...

How It Started

speaking to large groups of people. What do you do, by the way?"

She was wrong about the talents untried, I thought, because I *had* tried many different areas in the fashion business as well as other types of work, volunteer and paid, and I'd run out of ideas. When she mentioned the public eye, I thought she had probably read my mind—I *had* done work in those areas. But should I help Mary by answering Paul's question? Why not? So I mentioned that I was in the fashion business and advertising.

"She says she sees a lot of money around you," said Paul.

"Money?" I asked.

"Lotta money," said Mary herself. (Apparently she could speak a bit of English.) Should I believe this? I knew I would inherit some money eventually, but not "a lot." Nice as this was to hear, it could apply to many people.

After that dubious start, she made some predictions that I didn't take seriously because they sounded too good to be true: "If you write a book about your special knowledge, you will make a lot of money," she continued. "It would be an unusual book."

My only writing experience was rewriting a friend's essay in university. She got an "A" and I got a "B." (I'm not proud of either fact, but we had 35 hours of classes a week, and by the time we got to the library all the books were out.) As for special knowledge, all that I had at the time was about the fashion business.

Interesting, but hardly thrilling.

"You have been a spiritual teacher in many past lives," Paul said. "What religion are you now?"

"None," I replied, "I've been an agnostic since I walked out of the Anglican Church when I was 13, a year after I was confirmed." But I was thinking simultaneously that maybe the reason I left is because I'd had enough of organized religion in past lives. This was the first time I ever thought about reincarnation.

Pamela Evans

I left the Church because I found it boring. My parents weren't churchgoers, and only some of my friends. Also, the minister lived right behind us and, though friendly, was a heavy drinker even at social gatherings. (As an all-knowing teenager, I thought he wasn't up to his job, or any other.) One day I just walked away after yet another confusing service, thinking to myself, "If I live by the Golden Rule, surely I can't go too far wrong."

I might have found Mary's suggestion of spiritual lives or even past lives amusing, but oddly enough it struck a chord somewhere inside and I kept my mouth shut for a change. I'd think about it.

Then came the first big one.

"You will never inherit your mother's diseases... you have strong feet and legs... you will never be in a wheelchair."

How could she know my greatest fear? I'd never told a soul how frightened I was of "inheriting" my mother's Alzheimer's or her alcoholism or diabetes. I sat up straighter—probably with my mouth open.

One of the names I'd given her was my husband's. Running the finger of her left hand over it, Mary said, "Your husband loves the water... but he must be careful in the water... with the tops of his legs." Dave, my husband, would live and die on a boat if he could have his way. He'd been in a naval officer's training course in university and still took annual boat trips with his buddies. He'd also just completed a scuba diving course. Maybe that's where the danger might be.

Shaking her finger at me, Mary said, "Your husband must not take on a fourth partner. Business is going to drop off severely. He won't have enough work for a new person." She repeated the statement when she sensed it hadn't sunk in. "Things are going to be tight for a while," she added, and fixed me with those eyes, making sure I got this message loud and clear. She had already told me that he "practiced law but didn't go to court." Since that was correct, I began to have the

How It Started

feeling that this might be too. I hadn't known that Dave and his two partners had been talking about taking on a student in their office as a fourth partner because business was booming. As it turned out, he and I had seven years of serious financial hardship that started later in the month when his largest client, a builder, announced that he wasn't going to build houses that year for fear of a coming recession.

Before moving her finger down to my daughter Lisa's name, Mary closed her eyes again for a few seconds, opened them and said, "Somebody close to you... an older woman... has a constriction," and she made fists to show me. "She will have crisis in five months... I see her eyes go black."

"It's probably my mother," I said, "She's been sick for about three years."

"No, seben," said Mary. Seven years?

My mother passed out in her bedroom five months later, falling and hitting her head on her dressing table. Dad and I thought it was just from drinking too much, but a later test confirmed a stroke.

Mary described the personalities of my two children better than I could have, and gave me general reassurances about their futures, with one exception. "Your son will be a self-made millionaire... he will make you very proud." That statement sustained me over the years.

"Your Daddy is sick... he must go to the doctor," she said, pointing to her lower abdomen, side and ribs. I told him right away but it was two weeks before he finally took my advice. It was bad news—prostate cancer had advanced to what is called stage "D", and had spread to his bones.

(I had heard that the worst cancer pain of all was in the terminal stage of bone cancer. My heart ached for him. The next time I would see Mary was following the diagnosis. "Will he suffer terrible pain, Mary?" "No," she said, "he will fight this disease because his constitution is strong and then he will sleep away for three days." She put her hands to one side of her face, palms together. "No pain... he has suffered enough in this life." He lived for nine years and died peacefully after a three-day coma. His doctor assured me he was in no pain.)

May my mother forgive me for mentioning such a personal matter, but I feel the need to show how remarkable Mary's gift was. "This older woman close to you... is destroying herself [with alcohol, over the past forty years]. You must never feel guilty," Mary went on. "She is childishly irrational... it is not your fault."

I couldn't have described my mother more accurately even though I had lived with her and tried to figure out what made her tick all my life. Tears came. I sat there stunned again. Forty years of guilt lifted off my shoulders with one simple statement. What psychiatrist could have done that?

Mary folded one of my hands over the other and placed her hands on mine. The reading was over.

"Mary wants to know if she can say a prayer for you," said Paul.

"Sure," I said. If Mary thought a prayer might help, that would be fine—she obviously knew more about matters of the spirit than I did. After the reading I'd just had, I felt like I was in the presence of real magic. That thunderbolt started a quest for knowledge about reincarnation and psychic ability that is as insistent now as it was then: I was still an agnostic that day, but soon became a true believer in a Creator and a divine plan.

Mary prayed silently. Then, looking up, said goodbye and smiled for the first time. She said something to Paul who turned to me. "Mary wants to know why you are wearing a square bracelet."

I shrugged in my mesmerized stupor. "Just to be different, I guess."

Creaking out of the cramped chair, I fished for my money. (Ten dollars for the extra-ordinary information I'd just heard was the best deal ever. Imagine knowing I would never have Alzheimer's disease, particularly when it seemed to run in the family.)

How It Started

Saying goodbye to Mary was frustrating. I wanted to tell her how fascinated I was and ask her how she did it. Where did she get the information? Was it voices, pictures or what? She simply nodded and remained seated.

The black cat left when we did. "She comes every day at four to be fed," Paul explained. They had no idea where it came from.

☙ ❧

Dave raised a skeptical eyebrow when he heard my report. He was curious, but his interest perked up when I told him what Mary had said about his law practice, and her warning about his legs.

"How did she know about the fourth partner?" he asked. "You must have told her something to give her the idea."

"Absolutely not." (The first of many such arguments with other skeptics.) "It was the first thing she mentioned about you. All I'd done before that was write down your name and birthday as Paul told me to when I sat down in front of her." She had also mentioned that Dave didn't go to court in his practice. No patronizing looks this time and when I asked him if he'd like to give it a try, he said, "Sure, why not? But don't tell anybody until I see for myself." This was when he reminded me that he'd read a book about Edgar Cayce, the most famous and most highly documented psychic in America. Dave was going to see Mary, but "prove it" was still his middle name.

Following this first meeting with Mary, I began to read about reincarnation. When I discussed it with Dave, he insisted, with his legal training, that I be careful and accurate with my facts before going public—even at cocktail parties—if I didn't want to sound like a flake. This was good advice: nobody can embellish a story better than I.

After he went to bed, I started to make notes. Mary didn't tape her readings as later psychics did. Trying to remember all the details, I sat back and pondered the extraordinary experience I'd had that day.

My secret fears, Dave's love of the water, his occupation and personality, my children's personalities and appearance, all these Mary had clearly described. She was wrong about the length of my mother's illness, I thought, and only time would tell about the other predictions she'd made. How accurate were psychics on the whole, or did they vary in their skills? Were they born with the gift? How seriously should I take her warnings, and how much hope should I have about the rest of her predictions?

Next morning, I didn't have time to think about the reading until I got to my office. I was a freelance fashion illustrator and writer, and used Dave's office and phone number for my business. (The price was right!)

Sitting at my drawing board, I still couldn't understand the significance of "seben years" in connection with my mother's illness. Suddenly it dawned on me that she had exhibited the first obvious signs of diabetes *exactly seven years previously*. She was in Florida when it happened and had to come home early. The hair at the back of my neck prickled and I reached for the phone to make another appointment.

Mary could tell you about anybody alive or "in spirit," as most psychics call life after death. It's one thing to read my mind, if that's what she was doing, but quite another to give accurate information I hadn't previously known about other people.

The more I thought about the reading, the more awed I became of Mary's abilities, and the more curious about what else she could do. That first reading was just the tip of the iceberg of her psychic abilities. She was born with these gifts and so were her mother and grandmother.

I could hardly wait for another reading. Mary was available at two o'clock on Friday afternoon, three

How It Started

days away. I planned to write the names of my mother, father, and late grandfather, to see what she could tell me. I'd adored my grandfather and still missed him thirty years later.

               ✢ ✢

At the second reading I was much more relaxed. When I entered the room, Mary was sitting and rocking in the same place. This time, I noticed a few more details. Standing diagonally across from the door was a colored statue of the Virgin Mary. I was surprised. Roman Catholicism, which the statue suggested, was an odd mix with a psychic consultant considering the unfortunate relationship the two had shared in the past.

    Settling myself on the awkward chair again, I glanced at the wall above Paul's head. Hanging there was a handmade, multi-colored rug. Paul, noticing my glance, told me the story behind it.

    "A wealthy businessman, a regular client of Mary's, gave it to her after she warned him not to drive his car because there was something dangerously wrong with it," explained Paul. "She told him he could have a serious accident if he didn't get it fixed right away. The man *did* take the warning seriously because he knew Mary, but he had to drive the following day. So he drove slowly, and suddenly the right front wheel fell off. He wasn't hurt even though he ended up in the ditch.

    "Mary helps the police, too," Paul went on. "A few years ago, three women were murdered in Strathroy [a small town near London]. One day, some family members of the third lady came to Mary to see if she could help find the murderer. Women in the town were afraid to go out. They couldn't find the killer. Mary told the relatives that the police would find the killer next week. He would be driving a truck with *animal blood mixed with human blood*. The following week, just as Mary had said, they caught the murderer. He worked at the slaughterhouse in Strathroy and drove his own truck. They tested the blood and, sure enough," Paul said proudly, "*they found two kinds of blood* just as Mary had said they would. And he was convicted of all three murders."

Mary had been "tuning in" during these stories and was ready to start the reading. The three names I wanted to hear about were written on the pad between us. Since the first reading, I had read *The Sleeping Prophet*, by Jess Stearn, a well-known journalist. It was the story of Edgar Cayce and explained reincarnation and many other aspects of life after death. So, armed with a tiny bit of information about this mysterious business, I asked, "Can you bring my late grandfather's spirit into the room, Mary?"

"I try," said Mary herself, and bowed her head. Long seconds later she looked up and said, "Ya, he here," and pointed over her left shoulder. "He say, 'Hi, Pammer.'" That was my grandfather's nickname for me. It had to be him. I couldn't sense anything different, but no one else had ever called me "Pammer."

"He's been dead a long time," said Mary, placing her fingers on my grandfather's name. "I see diamonds and gold around him." He had owned a jewelry store.

He was also a Christian Scientist and wouldn't go to a doctor. "What did he die from?" I asked.

"Heart trouble," she said, "There were no drugs in those days to help him. The heart trouble was made worse by some business he felt guilty about and by stress caused by his wife." (He'd hated the government, I remembered, and when I asked about his relationship with my grandmother, my father said, "He could never do the right thing for her as far as pleasing her. He did his best, but it was never enough.")

"I see an explosion," continued Mary, "and people being killed... and I see a boat roll over... two tragedies... hurt him very much." (His son, my Uncle Jack, said later, "Oh sure, Dad's uncle was killed when the old city hall floor collapsed. And the boat story was probably the day the riverboat *Victoria* rolled over,

How It Started

killing half the people on board. I think he did lose a friend on that.")

※ ※

Two days later, during a party, I told some friends what Mary had said. They were fascinated. One of them suggested I get in touch with Hilary Alderson if I wanted to learn more. Hilary had been studying this sort of thing for years while running a very successful cheese shop and restaurant.

We met for coffee the next day at "Say Cheese." Hilary was a pixyish woman in her forties with short salt and pepper hair. Her soft voice blended easily with an English accent. Later in our friendship, she told me her estranged husband, whom she knew was gay before she married him, tried to attack her in the kitchen with a knife. He left her with a young son, no money and a fledgling business to run.

"Could you tell me a bit about reincarnation?" I asked.

"Certainly," said Hilary, straightening up in her chair as if to give it her all. She was always enthusiastic about *anything* metaphysical, as I learned during many lunches over the years. "You see, each human soul chooses to live several lifetimes in different roles in order to experience every facet of human existence, one way or another. A soul can't be truly compassionate unless it has suffered the same experience itself, good or bad. We are *all* in school during each physical lifetime, in order to learn various skills and understandings that we have chosen, before we are born, to experience.

"We choose our parents, our friends and our problems. We can't blame anybody but ourselves for what we go through—that's a cop-out," she explained. "Some people have their toughest lessons early in life to get them out of the way, while young souls usually choose to have their 'dessert first'—an easy early life— and experience their tough lessons later. An old soul is a highly evolved one; it has lived many lifetimes and has learned its lessons well. You can recognize an old soul by its wisdom in life's decisions. We all know people who are smart but not very wise, and vice versa," Hilary said, "and we both know children who are old or wise beyond their years.

"The knowledge from former lives remains forever in the subconscious and emerges as intuition, hunches or talents in this one. Famous composers, such as Mozart, are examples of talents returned at an extremely young age.

"We're all the products of our past lives, both male and female, and we carry the positive and negative aspects of these experiences with us forever," said Hilary. "What we do with our lives is what's important, not necessarily how much we achieve."

"That makes sense to me," I said. "In fact, it makes a lot more sense than a lot of other stuff that I've heard. But how can you prove it? I'm not questioning what you've said... I guess I just want to have an argument ready for whenever someone challenges me on the subject."

"It's hard to prove," said Hilary, "but there are a few cases you'll read about in the Edgar Cayce book on reincarnation where Cayce gives information about recent past lives that checked out through records still available. In one case, Cayce directed a man to a tombstone from a past life and he found it. You know, Pam, one lifetime doesn't make any sense at all."

After an hour of conversation, I left with a list of books and a date to meet her for lunch the next week.

❧ ☙

I arrived at Mary's door again. My third visit. This time, I was hoping she could tell me something about my past lives.

Paul met me at the back door and stayed in the waiting room for a chat since Mary's current customer spoke German.

How It Started

"How old was Mary when she first knew she was psychic?" I asked him.

"Five years old," said Paul. "One day she told her grandma there was a man outside the door, but her grandma told her she was crazy.

"'But Grandma, there *is* a man out there,' Mary said. "Finally her grandma opened the door and sure enough there was a man standing there."

"How did you happen to come to London, Paul?"

"We lived in Berlin before we came here, but we lived so close to the Wall that we could hear the shooting all the time. Mary hated it, so we decided to come here. We did have some friends here, but they're gone now. That was ten years ago," he said. "And Mary was working too hard. She gave readings from ten o'clock in the morning until ten o'clock at night, every night of the week. She was getting too old for that. You know, Pam, Mary is seventy-five years old in August. Isn't that amazing?" I nodded.

"Mary used to read for the Shah of Iran, you know," he continued, "and Saroya still writes to us. I'll show you a letter if you don't believe me. She just writes to let us know how she is."

"Tell me more about Mary; I love these stories."

"One time," he said, hardly stopping for breath, "some people came from the United States to see Mary. Their son had been abducted and they wanted to find him. Mary was just new in the country then, so she asked them to bring her a map of North America. She put her finger on their boy's location. They went out west to the place where Mary had said he'd be, and they brought him home. The following week they sent Mary the nicest 'thank you' letter. Mary gets all kinds of letters, you know," he said, "from all over the world."

Mary's German-speaking client left and for the third time I eased into the tiny chair. I heard good news and bad news this time. The bad news was there were so many deaths around me that it made the hair on Mary's arms stand up. She showed me her arms where the hair was standing on end. (Nine years later we had four deaths in three years: Dave's brother, his mother and my parents.)

"You and your daughter were friends in Egypt a thousand years ago," said Mary. "You and your husband were married to each other in Atlantis ten thousand years ago."

"Wow." I thought, that certainly explains why my daughter looks like Nefertiti in profile. (In high school, she moaned about the appearance of her nose. No amount of persuasion that it was elegant would convince her she wasn't cursed. When I told her what Mary had said and she later heard it for herself from Mary, she changed her attitude—and saved us the cost of plastic surgery. She really does look like one of the profiles you'd see in an Egyptian tomb. From then on, she would walk around the house with a towel wrapped around her head to show off her "Egyptian nose." Whether or not the past life was a fact, the information gave her self-esteem a boost and made all our lives easier until the next teenage crisis.)

"You're going to get a new job... right away," said Mary. Good, I thought, but I put it out of my mind for the rest of the reading.

As I wheeled into our driveway after the reading, I could see Lisa leaning out the front door, saying something I couldn't quite catch the first time.

"Mom, there's a man from Toronto on the phone asking for you," she repeated.

The man was Peter Gzowski, a well known radio "star" calling to ask me if I'd like to sell advertising for a new magazine starting up in London. He'd heard my name from mutual friends who knew I'd been connected with advertising. I thanked him, and explained I'd love to work on the magazine but on the editorial side. He offered me the job of fashion editor. The new job Mary had just told me about was now a fact.

How It Started

Three more readings helped me confirm certain information. By now, I felt comfortable enough with Mary and Paul to ask about some information I'd been reading about the spirit world.

"Don't be afraid of ghosts or spirits," she assured me. "Many spirits of dead people gather around this house because they know I can help them."

I'd read that ghosts are troubled spirits of dead people who don't realize they're dead and have unfinished business with our world. These longings won't let them follow their proper course of development. "They don't know how to follow the 'light,'" said Paul. "Mary can talk to them and send them on their way."

"What does a spirit look like, Mary?" I asked. "Do you see the whole person or just an outline or what?"

"Always different," said Mary directly. "Sometimes I feel them around me and they talk to me. Sometimes I see them clearly, just like you and I look, and sometimes, I see just faces, even in the trees out there," she said, and pointed out the window. "I tell them that they're dead, and that it's time to follow the white light to the next world." The "white light" was mentioned in several books I'd read, and by now more readers have likely heard something about "white light" if they've read about near-death experiences.

Once, during a reading when Paul was called to the phone, Mary said, "You go on cruise," and picked up the pencil.

"I can't imagine that, Mary. My husband *hates* getting dressed up. He's always said he'd never want to subject himself to that torture.

"No, different cruise." And she started to draw a squiggly triangle with two lines flowing to the left at the base of it, and then another triangle at the right end. "See," she said, "different boat." I hated to disappoint her but I couldn't figure out what she was drawing. Three years later, at eleven-thirty in the evening, good friends called us to see if we could be ready by Monday to go on an eleven-day cruise down the St.

Lawrence River with them. The couple with whom they'd bought the trip at a theatre auction couldn't go at the last minute.

We had a dream trip that only cost us $250 dollars each for eleven days of perfect weather. Mary had been trying to draw a lake freighter that day.

My days were numbered with Mary and Paul. They were leaving London for Vancouver Island, where they owned property. I went for one last reading.

"If you write a letter, I send you reading," said Mary.

"Mary says she knows your palm so well, now, that she can easily read you from our new home," said Paul. "She can get vibrations from your handwriting." I later learned that handwriting is "brain writing" and when Mary pressed her fingers on certain locations in my palm, she was touching the energy flow that was connected to a particular part of my soul's energy.

Shortly before they left, I bumped into Mary at the supermarket as we rounded the same corner. It was the day after the assassination attempt on the Pope. Mary put her hand on my arm. "Pope… no good… conspiracy," she said.

I filed this away in my head and enjoyed having inside "astral" information when the rest of the world was still puzzled about the attempt. Time has proven her right, it seems.

Mary and Paul sold their home in September and headed west. I was going to miss her. There were many troubled times ahead for us in the next seven years, during which time I would have given anything just to hold Mary's hands and hear her insight and predictions of silver linings.

Mary's first prediction by phone from Vancouver, with Paul's help, had some surprises. I'd written a letter with money enclosed for a reading. When I hadn't heard after four weeks I called. They had just received my letter the previous day, Paul explained, so they

How It Started

gave me a reading over the phone. Paul simply repeated whatever Mary said, as usual.

"Mary says to watch out for 'danger around your car,'" said Paul. I had an old TR-6 that was rusty right through. Three months later, it started needing new parts regularly, and one day, while making a right turn, the left front of the car collapsed about eight inches with a bang. The left front ball-joint broke and I could have been killed if I'd been on the highway when it happened.

"This is not the time to sell your house," said Mary, "Later on, changes in zoning laws and special buildings near you will raise the value of your property." She had never seen our house and didn't know where we lived. Today, we have not only massive subdivisions on all sides, but also a huge mall and 12 theatres at our main corner, four blocks away. The other two sides of the main intersection near us have two large areas of stores. (This is 20 years after that prediction.)

Her January letter frightened and depressed me.

"Pam, I told you to go for a checkup before, and I'm telling you again to go. Your gallbladder shows weakness."

My gallbladder! I'd never had an attack, but maybe the heartburn waking me up in the night for the last year or so was really a gallbladder problem. I called our family doctor and told him the symptoms.

"Why didn't you tell me this sooner," he asked, "and how long have you had these symptoms?"

"About a year or two," I answered, starting to feel nervous instead of silly.

"It sounds like gallbladder to me," said the doctor, "but it could be anything. I'll arrange tests right away. Meanwhile, cut out all fats. You don't want to have an attack while you're waiting for the test results,"

The thought of an operation and a six-week recovery period depressed me because I couldn't afford to lose even one client. Over the next three days, I went through the tests he'd arranged: ultrasound, X-rays, blood tests, the works.

Nothing showed up in the tests, but twenty-four hours after I cut out fatty foods, particularly cheese and potato chips, I slept through the night for the first time in ages. Only twice after that did I have any trouble: once, after eating a corned beef sandwich (I had no idea they were loaded with fat) and once after eating a handful of dry-roasted sunflower seeds (I'd let the "dry roasted" fool me).

So it appears that Mary saved me from years of discomfort and from a possible gallbladder attack down the road. I shake my head in amazement when I picture Mary sitting at her kitchen table three thousand miles away zeroing in on my gallbladder when all the expensive equipment at the medical center couldn't come up with the diagnosis that it wasn't functioning as it should.

≥ ≤

Mary had told my friend Polly that she was going to have a car accident but wouldn't be hurt.

"Can I avoid this accident?" asked Polly.

"No," said Mary. She explained to Polly that some things coming toward us are fixed, can't be changed no matter what, while other things sometimes can be changed if we change our behavior. (We choose the fixed events before we're born, according to the evidence.)

About a year later, Polly was stopped at a red light when she saw a car coming toward her from the opposite direction, sliding on the ice. She remembered Mary's warning and knew she wouldn't be hurt. She ducked sideways on the seat. The impact of the collision shortened her car by five inches—but Polly wasn't hurt.

≥ ≤

How It Started

During my first reading, Mary had said, "You will own two homes... one in the East on the water."

At that time, in 1980, even if our parents had died it wouldn't have been financially possible. But a series of circumstances—particularly the death of Dave's brother—made it feasible. Our small white villa in Florida is on the East Coast... on the water.

Mary also described our son's and daughter's future partners to them. Lisa, 20 at the time, was told that her husband would be finished with school and independent when they met. He would be five years older than she, and that he would own a house on a corner lot. When they met, said Mary, he would feel like he'd been punched in the stomach from the effect of the meeting.

I was inadvertently part of this destined meeting. Lisa had just returned from three months in Europe and needed a job. Her only job experience at the time was bartending. I knew the owner of a downtown seafood bistro, near my office, where I regularly lunched. Convincing Lisa to join me for lunch to meet the owner for a possible job wasn't easy. She wasn't in the mood to work yet. But, since I still outweighed her, I won.

Her future husband, Glenn, waited on us, and told Lisa later that the minute he saw her *he felt like he'd been punched in the stomach*. He also owned a house on a corner and is five years older. The only thing Mary *didn't* say was that he would be married with three children when they met! Still, he and Lisa were married eight years after they first met, ten years after the prediction.

Twenty years after Mary's prediction regarding our son Gray's future mate, he finally met her—at age 37. Mary told him that she would be older and previously married. (She's four years older and had been married before.). She would be small and dark, and her short, common name would begin with an "A". She's short and dark. Her name is Ann. And she would be the one who started the relationship. "And I did," said Ann.

When Gray came to tell us about her before we met, he said, "Mom, it's just like we've known each other for ever."

Whenever I think about the years of lonely wandering our son had experienced, I'm in awe that he finally met the woman Mary had described so long ago.

Both our children now know that their mates are meant to be lifetime partners, and, thanks to Mary's (and later Marge's) information, they know they've known each other in previous lives. This understanding could make the inevitable problems in marriage seem more like speed bumps in life rather than brick walls.

☙ ❧

Looking back, I know it was no accident that I went to an excellent psychic for my first visit. If I'd gone to one that was less gifted, I might have shrugged off the reading and never bothered to go again or learn about unseen forces at all. I used to think how much I would have missed if Mary hadn't started the quest. And how lucky I was to have gone to her first. Luck had nothing to do with it I learned later.

A few years after that first reading with Mary, another psychic said, *"Whenever you need help, the best person will be there to help you."* Mary was there to help me when I was ready for spiritual growth, it seems.

"We review our days," Joseph Campbell once wrote, and we notice "how encounters and events that appeared at the time to be accidental became the crucial structuring features of an unintended life story."

2
My Bizarre Spiritual Background And Other Events

My family sought salvation in a variety of ways... from "rich old lady cults" to solace in a bottle of gin. But they all taught me something spiritual or philosophical whether they realized it or not.

Grandma (Mother's Side)

"What are those purple pictures hanging on the wall, Grandma?" was my first of a long line of spiritual questions to come over the next sixty years.

My grandmother, who had been brought up in the Methodist Church, examined the Christian Science faith as well before joining a "rich old lady" cult—as the family referred to it behind her back. It called itself the "I Am." She papered her bedroom walls with long plastic-covered "I Am" posters—mainly mauve—in which rays of golden light emanated from ethereal figures gazing heavenward. These figures usually pointed a torch at God and wore wings. (According to my aunt, she would only wear mauve or yellow clothing, and insisted on driving yellow cars exclusively.)

Her religious pursuit was probably my earliest exposure—at age four—to anything spiritual. From the day of my first question, my precocious interest in spiritual matters prodded me to open a mental file of observations on matters of belief that surfaced in my life from time to time.

The rest of the family said grandma was "with the birds," whenever she sang her way around the house. She never learned to boil an egg and was lucky enough to have a cook. So she had time to pursue "whatever got her through the night," as Frank Sinatra once said.

One of her earlier "groups" met in a downtown classroom. Grandpa reported to anyone listening that he was taking Alice to "save the world for democracy."

It wasn't funny to Grandma.

Eventually, she set up a small meeting room on the third floor of her home. Mauve walls displayed rows of plastic-covered posters. A painted gold podium and rows of cream-colored bridge chairs faced each other. In the corner stood a cream-colored piano scattered with purple-printed music. Beside it, on a small table, sat a record player with a stack of purple records.

Grandma thought I was wonderful, so I hung around her a lot as a kid. Two months after I got my driver's license, she let me drive her all the way into Manhattan (about 500 miles). Backing into a tree while trying to turn around was my only mishap in the long trip. "Oh, that's nothing to worry about, dear," said Grandma, "I do that all the time." I loved her attitude. Because of it, I was willing to put up with her curious beliefs to be in her company.

In 1954, how many grandmothers handed their grandchild a book about flying saucers? Even though I knew her beliefs were eccentric, I read it and thought, *why couldn't there be other beings somewhere else?* Others in the family refused to read it and just shrugged at Grandma's crazy notions.

I loved the possibility that other worlds might exist.

Recently, I learned that Grandma often talked to a younger cousin about communicating with people from Venus. One day, while I was visiting her cottage—a teenager with nothing better to do—I picked up one of the purple books to skim. The spiritual message baffled me, something about rays and levels of existence, but gradually I was aware that I was experiencing some sort of physical reaction as I read it. Not exactly a "rush to the loins," but at some level—even at that age—I suspected it was the next best thing. (I'd already read a sexy scene in a Daphne DuMaurier novel, so I knew how *that* kind of reaction felt.)

    I had to stand up, take a deep breath and walk around before finishing the chapter. The writing had a powerful rhythm that rose in waves, each one stronger and more urgent than the last, creating a tension in me until the climax at the end of the chapter. There was no sexual language, but the effect was impressive. That sort of writing, I gather, was the genteel turn-on in those days.

    That reading experience was my introduction to the concept of a *dual purpose* paralleling the obvious message. It planted a seed of suspicion about the hidden intention of this religion. Was the pseudo-sexy literature a lure for older people with money who had nothing better to do? Or was I jumping to conclusions? Another thought to ponder.

    Near the end of her life, my husband had to kick a young man out of her house. He was involved in her cult and had come to "visit" her. Until then, the few men I'd met in her group were shadowy figures—usually husbands or sons. Their waxy skin, limp handshakes and lack of conversation steered me clear of them.

    The family worried that she'd hand over some of her jewelry sooner or later (and suspected the visitor might talk her into donating the rest). By this time, she had early Alzheimer's disease and really was "with the birds." She regularly left the house loaded with expensive jewelry. She also donated large sums of money to the group whenever they asked—and they asked frequently, as I'd learned from my observation post under the grand piano.

She never forgave my grandfather for dividing his estate equally among the children and her when he died. But he was no fool. He knew what would have happened if he'd left it all to her.

This probable—if it had continued—fleecing by a religious organization added a new element of suspicion to my list.

Recently, I stumbled on some books in our local New Age bookstore that were printed in purple. After skimming a few pages, I put them back on the shelf, and wondered later if cults like my grandmother's were mingling their literature with regular New Age information. A disturbing thought.

Grandpa (Mother's Side)

Christian Science was the religion that fulfilled my beloved grandfather. But he wouldn't talk about it.

Eavesdropping, during yet another family gathering at my grandparents' home—from my customary place under the grand piano—I learned that Christian Scientists never went to the doctor. Instead, they prayed for healing.

(I also accumulated the opinions some of the adults held regarding other family members' beliefs. That information joined the list too. I realized that each new round of martinis produced increasingly memorable remarks.)

For years, I thought the song *Carry Me Back to Old Virginny* was a Christian Science hymn. Grandpa always sang it as he walked around the house combing the five remaining strands of hair sideways over his dome.

He was so prejudiced against Catholics that, as a big candy lover who kept a box of chocolates under his bed at all times, he refused to eat Laura Secord chocolates because that was her religion. But when his

My Bizarre Spiritual Background

only son married a Catholic, he didn't object. He never mentioned Catholicism again and treated his new daughter-in-law like his own.

Grandpa not only taught me to live by the Golden Rule, but also that a guilty conscience was the "best thing in the world for the jewelry business."

Grandpa believed in mind-over-matter and didn't drink. One evening, some of his friends decided he needed a few strong ones—so the story goes. Apparently he drank them all under the table, walked away under his own steam—and drove home. *That's mind over matter!*

"I'm going to beat the man that made the game," he declared frequently. And, "everything in moderation," was another firm conviction—one I've had occasion to remember, after the fact.

No one in the family knew what illness did my Grandfather in at age 65. He had died suddenly, after complaining he was tired.

Mary told me 30 years later that, stress caused by his wife contributed to heart trouble that caused his death.

Why would my otherwise practical and intelligent grandfather not have gone to a doctor who might have helped him live longer?

My list was getting longer. Grandpa's belief seemed to interfere with his good judgement. This fact as well as other friends' "impaired" decisions based on religious belief that I witnessed began early to turn me off about organized religion.

Grandpa died when I was thirteen. It was my first loss of a loved one. As I swallowed my tears at his funeral, I had a strong feeling that he was the only one in the family who might have helped me get a start in life. I was right.

Pamela Evans

My Step-Grandfather (Father's Side)

Grandpa "Mac" was a frail, gentle Irishman and a Protestant. He'd designed religious monuments in Ireland before he'd become an architect. He was living and working in Detroit when he met my recently divorced grandmother. Then he'd lost his job from poor health.

Bad health had plagued him all his life until we met, and continued to for as long as I knew him.

In contrast to the grand home, gardens and lifestyle of my other grandparents, he lived a modest and thoughtful life. He and my grandmother carefully tended their tiny bungalow with its postage-stamp backyard and aquarium-sized fishpond. He fed songbirds outside the breakfast nook window—and taught me their names. In the summer he'd talk to the birds through the open casement window, and the birds chatted back.

I loved visiting them just as much as my other grandparents. And I was their *only* grandchild.

Grandpa earned small change designing tombstones (and loved it when I watched him fine-tuning a scroll or a letter in a name) in his basement workshop.

We would sit on the grass beside the pond while he rolled his own cigarettes and told me about his life in Ireland. As I got older, I sensed that he wanted to tell me his feelings about religion—without actually preaching. He knew about the unusual mixture of beliefs in my mother's family and probably guessed that I was drifting rudderless among many approaches to understanding life and God.

One day, by the pond, he said, "Pammy, I want to tell you something. I designed about ten religious figures for a particular monastery in Ireland. So I spent a lot of time supervising their placement and suggesting other locations if I thought they might be better. It took three years to complete the whole job. By then I knew

My Bizarre Spiritual Background

several of the priests and nuns quite well. They knew I wasn't Catholic, but they seemed to like me. One day, two of the nuns led me down some stairs to the basement. Taking me to a far corner, they pointed to an opening in the floor. I looked down at the pit below. It was full of quick lime, they said—and baby's bones." I shuddered.

He'd obviously drawn his own conclusions about the bones, and I—from that moment—began to draw mine. Not all is what it appears to be, I learned that day.

After we'd talked about this for a while he said, "I want to give you something that, I hope, will remind you of me and help you in life."

In the house he handed me a small brass statue of three crouching "joined at the hip" monkeys. The left one was covering its mouth, the middle one its eyes and the right monkey was holding its hands over its ears. "They're saying, 'Speak no evil, see no evil, hear no evil,' he said. "Pammy, if you mind those three things, you don't need any formal religion."

One morning, Grandpa died while watching his birds. The evening of his funeral I sat and thought about his life. The thought of his gentle but limited life started a surge of tears of despair. How could such a kind and unassuming man have such a difficult life of constant illness that forced him to leave his job... no children of his own... no money to enjoy life in spite of his education and talents... and no recognition for his ability? I furiously pounded a pillow over the unfairness of it all.

What was the point of his life?

Now that I understand reincarnation, I know he'll have another life, another chance at being appreciated. I can think of him again with pure pleasure.

A Christening

My parents and I (age five) were visiting friends in a nearby town for the christening of their child. I was too young to remember the service itself, which took place in their house. But I clearly remember the father of the child rushing past the room I was in, with a bowl of water—just before the event. He glanced at the small group of us and quipped that he mustn't spill the "holy water." I was shocked that such a nice man could make fun of something so serious. But no thunderbolt came down from Heaven. And furthermore, one of the other adults laughed.

It was okay to kid around about God.

A Catholic Christening

My Catholic friend's mother had her third baby, a girl named Joscelyn, when I was about nine. I loved feeding and caring for a real baby and hung around the household to hold her as often as I could.

Her christening, at about three weeks of age, was noteworthy to me for one reason: at the conclusion of the service, the priest announced that the baby's sins had now been washed away with the baptismal water.

What sins, I wondered? What could this dear little baby have done that was so bad? Was God that strict? Or was he just hard on Catholics?

Something kept me from asking any questions at the time. The memory of that christening still rests uneasily in my mind, over fifty years later. Would a just and loving God inflict sins on an innocent baby? Not as far as I was concerned that day—and I still feel that way.

Zero Population Growth

My Catholic friend was a kind and gentle person who adored her husband beyond the usual affection that I'd witnessed between adults to date. She never

My Bizarre Spiritual Background

discussed anything that wasn't pleasant, and flattered everyone she met.

But she didn't hesitate to voice her strong opinion one morning several years ago. The subject was my role in a radio broadcast the previous evening. The location was our local drugstore.

I'd been interviewed, as president of our local chapter of Zero Population Growth, about the serious problem of overpopulation. Nowhere in the program had I mentioned abortion. It played no part in my crusade.

Shortly after saying hello, she firmly established her disappointment at my role in the interview, summing it up with, "I never thought a friend of *mine* would do a thing like that."

The last time I'd heard such a putative guilt-producing remark, I was in grade eight, and my mother had just found a sex textbook in my sweater drawer.

That encounter made me bristle at the arrogance and elitism of organized religion. I don't appreciate a remark directed at me that indicates the speaker assumes not only that his or her belief is superior, but that mine is wrong.

While president of Zero Population Growth, I had diligently researched the dangers of overpopulation. One segment of information I'll never forget reading concerned the interconnection of all ecosystems. The more I thought of this "rather well-thought-out" chain reaction, the more impressed I was with the great mind that had thought it up in the first place. Even though I'd studied botany and zoology, I hadn't connected the dots in my mind with *who* might have thought out all the systems and physical characteristics we were studying in the first place. I'm still in awe of that great production we call Nature.

I think the door that opened in my mind, as a result of my research, beckoned me to learn more about natural laws. Certain belief in a supreme mind began to grow stronger as I accumulated more knowledge—

resulting in the conclusion that where there's a production of *any* kind, there *has* to be a producer.

Although science can tell us *what*—it still can't tell us *why*.

My Uncle (Mother's Brother)

My uncle didn't belong to any religious faith. Living by the Golden Rule was good enough for him. He wasn't criticized for not belonging to a religion. And he seemed quite content with life without any formal guidance. He was kind and friendly and well-liked.

Like Grandpa Mac, he taught me that a simple faith is all that's necessary to get through life.

Aunt Helen (Mother's Sister)

My favorite Aunt Helen—with whom I'd spent many cozy hours learning to crochet while listening to *The Romance of Helen Trent* and other daytime "soaps"— was experiencing a strange physical reaction whenever she attended church (another juicy morsel learned from under the piano).

She'd been brought up in the Anglican faith previously embraced by my grandparents. But she had what I would now call an "old-soul" wisdom about her that I loved. I didn't know about "old souls" then, but she seemed to flow wisely with the events in her life. She had a "you do your thing and I'll do mine" approach to people. "Don't worry, darlin', it'll all work out," she'd say, or, "It was meant to be." Everyone who knew her loved her. Married late in life, she had two children—her greatest wish.

Her down-to-earth good nature easily accepted attending the only church in the small town where she and her husband lived, even though it was a slightly different denomination.

But one day she started shaking in the middle of a service. The tremor stopped once she was outside.

My Bizarre Spiritual Background

Several more attempts to attend the Sunday service resulted in the same reaction. No one could figure it out.

She never attended church services again.

When her daughter and I were discussing the problem recently, I mentioned a possible explanation from my research into reincarnation, that some unhappy memory of a past-life religious experience might have been triggered by certain passages in the new service—or by the minister who conducted the service.

Hundreds of examples of similar situations have been recorded where someone has had an irrational reaction to a piece of music, a line in a movie or a certain passage in a religious service.

In her case, it certainly wasn't the flu.

Helen taught me to "bend like a willow, in dealing with life's lessons"...and that there is a God... and to have faith that things will go the way they're supposed to go.

Easter Sunday

I was about six when my father took me to my first church service. It was Easter Sunday. He'd sung in a choir in the Anglican Church when he was a child, but hadn't been to church since. My mother didn't come with us.

The pleasant atmosphere of organ music, rainbow-colored shafts of sunlight from the stained glass windows slanting through the motes of dust, and gigantic pewter chandeliers suspended from the vaulted ceiling soon took a back seat to fidgety boredom. The only other memory I have of that service is the geometric pattern printed by the dusty sole of my "Sunday shoe" on the pew in front of me—accompanied by a gentle admonishment from Dad to "sit up straight like a lady."

My lack of interest in the proceedings that day was just a foretaste of endless tedious hours I had yet to suffer in church, before I would finally have had enough.

My Mother

Alone in her room, my mother read a small religious pamphlet called *The Daily Word*. I suspected that frequently the perusal was accompanied by a glass of sherry. Neither appeared to give her much comfort. In fact, she emerged from her room far gloomier than when she had gone in.

Mother never discussed religion at all, at least in front of me. It was as if it were a taboo subject, like pregnancy was in the '40s and '50s.

Once, while I was taking confirmation classes, I asked her an innocent question about Jesus. She brushed me off in her flippant, defensive way with, "You'll just have to go to church more often to find *that* out."

I didn't know what I'd done wrong—but that was the last time I asked her about anything abstract.

I began to realize, even then, that she understood little about life, perhaps because she never read a book. Any wisdom that came from her had come from someone else. (I've since met lots of people like that.) She would leaf through women's magazines without reading any of the articles. Her only conversation was local news that she'd heard from her friends at the "club." She seemed to be seeking something, but I don't know what. The thought crossed my mind that what she really wanted was a "daddy" to look after her.

Around that time, I also began to suspect there was some emotional instability in her, an irrationality, but I wasn't sure and was afraid to suggest it to my father. I stopped asking questions because of her petulant answers and started to ask outsiders for any information my father couldn't supply.

In spite of her limitations, she taught me three valuable lessons. The first, "It's cruel to spoil a child, because *nobody* likes a pampered brat." The second, "Never say you hate someone—it will get you into trouble." And the third, "If you haven't got your health, you haven't got anything. Money's not *that* important."

Not such bad advice, but once I realized I was on my own, as far as philosophical guidance was concerned, I became a prodigious reader of self-help books and worried constantly that I might not learn information before I needed to use it.

I became old, very young.

My Friends: Sunday School, Church and Confirmation

My friends and I (usually five of us) went to Sunday school whenever our parents thought it might be a good idea. It was a random schedule, usually connected with rainy or cold Sundays, or our parents' need to recover from a late Saturday night.

I loved coloring the pictures, but never retained any of the Bible stories except that of Moses in the bulrushes. It intrigued me.

Once we outgrew Sunday school, we sporadically attended church. My only memories from those occasions were trying to stifle uncontrollable giggling, and receiving a bloody nose when my closest friend grabbed it to retaliate for something I'd done to her.

The next spiritual step, at age twelve, was to be confirmed (to become a member of the church). All five of us attended the same series of classes to gain this ranking. No wonder our local minister drank.

Church protocol was a mystery. I knew little about the church and—more uncomfortably—began to suspect that I didn't care. But, by the end of the sessions (we got away with enough right answers to get by) we were "confirmed." Dressed in white, we marched importantly up the aisle and became official members of the Anglican Church.

The Big Decision

For the year following our confirmation, I went to church by myself. It was lonely because my friends now usually accompanied their parents.

Going alone was a blessing in disguise. Without my friends to distract me, I was actually paying attention to the service. But no matter how hard I tried to pay attention, I learned nothing from the service. I began to hate the half-hour it took to get through the prayer book. It bored me to death. And the hymns, with too few exceptions, were ponderous. The droning sermons taught me nothing that I, as a thirteen-year-old, wanted to know. Could I stand listening to this for the rest of my life?

No.

Shuffling through the dead leaves on the way home from yet another meaningless service, I told myself that I thought I believed in God. And if there was one, and He knew that I lived by the Golden Rule, how far wrong could I go?

So, not having discussed my decision with anyone, I decided not to go back—ever.

My Children

Years later, I had a chat with my two children (ages twelve and thirteen at the time). "I'm feeling guilty that you two haven't *ever* been to Sunday school. I don't know what I believe about God or religion, but I think, if nothing else, it might make you more at ease at religious functions—and you'll be going to lots of those in your life—if you were even slightly familiar with one...."

"Mom," interrupted my daughter, "You've always taught us to live by the Golden Rule. What else do we need?"

Long pause from me. "You know what, Lisa, you're probably right. When you're older or have kids, you may decide that you want some formal religion. Sometimes organized religion can kick-start spiritual thinking; everyone needs something to bounce from or rebel against. But you can jump off that bridge when you come to it."

"By the way," I added, "you were both christened in the Anglican Church when you were about three months old. That means that you're members of the church. But you can undo that anytime, if you want. We only did the deed to pacify both grandmothers. I think it's wrong to attach a child to a church before he or she is old enough to understand what it's all about."

Summer Camp: An Astounded Agnostic

Sunday morning chapel service was mandatory at Camp Inawendawin (friendship, in Indian). The saving grace was the setting: a clearing in a grove of birch trees at the edge of a small northern lake in Canada.

The head counselor conducted the all-purpose Christian service. A large picture of Jesus, propped against the rustic podium, directed his blue-eyed gaze over the sinners—sitting cross-legged on groundsheets, yawning.

The flock generally paid no attention to Jesus or the head counselor as she chirped piously through the endless service. We usually remained sitting on our groundsheets to sing the chosen hymns.

On the Sunday in question, I was sitting on my groundsheet imagining the spectacle of a hundred rumps rising in the air at each hymn, if we'd had to stand to sing. And pondering my list of grievances with the head counselor, whom I, as a junior counselor, baited at every opportunity. She was lady-like, musically gifted, cheerful, thin and a perpetual student—every thing my mother had wanted me to be. I wanted to push her off the dock.

Then suddenly the first line of the most electrifying hymn I'd ever heard yanked my wandering attention to a halt.

Not having bothered to open the hymnbook to the right number, I scrambled through the pages to find the words. The first two lines had gone right through me. I'll *never* forget it.

> And did those feet in ancient time
> Walk upon England's mountains green?
> And was the holy Lamb of God
> On England's pleasant pastures seen?
> And did the countenance Divine
> Shine forth upon our clouded hills?
> And was Jerusalem builded here
> Among these dark Satanic Mills?
> Bring me my bow of burning gold!
> Bring me my arrows of desire!
> Bring me my spear! O clouds, unfold!
> Bring me my chariot of fire!
> I will not cease from mental fight
> Nor shall my sword sleep in my hand
> Till we have built Jerusalem
> In England's green and pleasant land.
> — William Blake

My throat closed and tears came. I was stunned and shivery. What was going on? How could such an opinionated agnostic be so shaken up by religious music? I hated religious music. But I'll never forget the moment I heard the *first four lines* of that magnificent hymn.

I think that most religious music infuriates me because I associate it with the inhumanities of some

My Bizarre Spiritual Background

religions—both in the past and present. But this beautiful hymn I eventually learned by heart and shivered whenever I thought of the words. Maybe some day I will learn their deeper meaning.

When I was so transfixed by the hymn that day, I later found, my subconscious memories from a past life had bypassed my conscious mind and had created a physical reaction.

William Blake belonged to one of the many secret societies that have preserved ancient spiritual information. Therefore he probably had access to manuscripts with what was secret information about Jesus.

And, years later, *three* different psychics would tell me that I had been a follower of Jesus—in secret—and knew about his trips to England.

Quo Vadis: The White Light

Around the same time that I heard the Hymn, my friends and I went to the current hit movie, *Quo Vadis*. Stuffing ourselves with popcorn, we admired Deborah Kerr (such a small waist!) and Robert Taylor (*so* sexy) and the flowing togas that hid a multitude of midnight snacks. The plot took a back seat to the costumes and sets that evening.

Toward the end of the movie, two of the leading characters were moving down a road when a white light appeared from the woods, a voice said, "Quo vadis...?" and gave them a message that I now can't recall.

I had to stop eating because my throat closed. The scene choked me up as much as Blake's hymn had, only this time my irreverent pals were with me. When the movie ended shortly after that scene, one of them remarked that I hadn't made any smart remarks about the "God scene." I couldn't, because I was afraid I was going to cry. I was truly speechless.

It was a magical scene and I'll never forget how the feeling lingered. It must have set off another memory of a previous lifetime during that period of history. But, in retrospect, I felt God had come close for a moment.

What's It Like To Die?

The only other movie that had a memorable spiritual scene—but in a different way—was the *Philadelphia Story*.

There was a scene where the father was explaining death to a child of six or so. He said to the child, "Do you remember when you were little and you fell asleep in the car at night and next morning you woke up in your own room?"

The child answered, "Yes."

"Well, that's what it's like to die. We go to sleep and wake up in another room."

This simple explanation made more sense than any other description I'd heard before. Or since.

Margaret and Sandy: A Lesson in Courage

Margaret, my mother's Scottish cleaning woman, was cheerful in spite of a homely appearance and a distressing domestic life. Her alcoholic husband had died soon after she started working for us. Then one of her two sons died in a work-related accident. That left her with a tiny frame house, one son who lived out of town, and a Down Syndrome daughter nicknamed Sandy.

From the age of seven, I was not only aware of her situation, but followed the unfolding particulars of her life at lunch each Friday.

As soon as I had my driver's license, I would drive her home at the end of the day. In the car, she cheerfully reminisced about people she'd worked for in

My Bizarre Spiritual Background

Scotland where she'd been trained as a maid. Sandy always ran out to greet her on the front lawn and clung to her all the way into the house.

That little scene choked me up every Friday for five years. Driving home, I pondered the unfairness of life and wondered how Margaret could be so cheerful in spite of her hard life while my mother, with her fur-lined existence, constantly whined and faced everything through the bottom of a glass.

Both Margaret and my mother developed Alzheimer's disease. Mom was the first to exhibit the signs. Margaret eventually couldn't work any more and disappeared from sight. I was busy with a job and a young family at the time.

Eventually, I heard she was in a convalescent home and, sometime later, that she'd died. Whenever I thought about her, I wondered who was looking after Sandy.

A few years ago, our local newspaper featured a heartwarming, full-page article about Sandy—and how well she was doing. The article described her life, the many friends she enjoyed, and how the support from a local agency gave her the freedom to live on her own in an apartment. The article mentioned that Margaret was in a nursing home at the time.

Three years after the article, I was returning home from a walk, when I bumped into Sandy. She was leaving her apartment to catch a bus. I hadn't seen her in thirty years.

I refreshed her memory and we chatted for a few minutes until her bus pulled up. Looking up at me through her bottle-bottom glasses, she said, "God bless you, my child."

Those words should have come from me, I thought, as I watched her climb awkwardly aboard.

A year later, while glancing at one of our national newspapers, I spotted a picture of Sandy under the heading "Lives Lived," a column that usually discusses personalities with an impressive list of accomplishments or contributions to society. The entire right-hand column of the back page had a write-up on Sandy's life until her recent death. The column was a remarkable tribute to the pleasure that Sandy had given to so many people by her cheerful friendliness and caring.

The old familiar sadness hit me, but this time it was short-lived. My subsequent understanding of reincarnation has taught me that even though Sandy's life was hard, her next life will be easier... that life is *ultimately* fair... and that death is simply a *comma* in the book of life.

Watching Sandy ecstatically hug her mother, so many years ago, started my deepest philosophical questioning. It began a personal quest to find evidence of universal justice.

I thought at the time that, if life isn't fair, what's the point of trying? Or of living?

The Bible Group

One day, over twenty years ago, while I still wandered in the wasteland of agnosticism, my regular tennis foursome sat down after a game to enjoy a cool drink. Before I'd even finished settling into my chair, Aline, one of the girls said, "I'm so much happier now that I've found Jesus."

Somebody *up there* clamped a hand over my big mouth, before I made a clever remark. I'd assumed that Aline was kidding. She was *not*.

That was my introduction to the existence of a "Bible thumping" assembly within our golf club. I hadn't been aware of it until then. The other two women in the tennis foursome were evidently part of it too. It quickly became apparent that they were serious about their commitment. I was outnumbered.

Could my opinionated agnosticism resist this target? No. But I did restrain my questions to thoughtful queries, such as, "How can you be sure that Jesus is God?"

My Bizarre Spiritual Background

By the time they'd finished trying to enlighten me, I suspect they had a profound interest in my spiritual welfare.

A month later, the group's leader (who'd probably been notified) called.

"Pam, I know that you're in the fashion business, so how would you like to come to lunch at the club, as my guest, to hear a *real* New York fashion model speak?"

"Thanks, Ginny. I'd love to."

The large dining room was packed with chattering women when I arrived for lunch the appointed day. I recognized at least half of them. Lunch was enjoyable. During dessert, the New York fashion model—eight months pregnant and married to a Denver Bronco quarterback—lumbered to her feet to spellbind us with fashion stories.

"I'm so happy I've found Jesus—praise the Lord."

Don't tell me, I groaned to myself. Why didn't I see it coming? Looking around to see other reactions, I knew there wasn't a kindred soul in the room. Everyone else was regarding the speaker with enchantment. How long can I listen to this nonsense, I wondered? Looking at my watch, I tried to guess how long I'd be trapped.

Ten chairs blocked me from the nearest exit.

Two factors kept me warming the seat: curiosity, and some semblance of breeding, instilled by my mother. My parents were well-known at the club, and some of Mom's friends were at the lunch.

There was no discussion of the fashion business whatsoever.

"How did you like it?" asked one of my Friday tennis buddies on the way out—looking a bit hesitant, I thought.

"Can't you see the smoke coming out of my ears?"

Word got back to the chief. Next morning, Ginny called and apologized. "I had no idea she wasn't going to talk about the fashion business."

Right.

My investigation into the group's membership fished up a surprisingly long list of familiar names. This was a fundamentalist group with Pentecostal and Baptist roots, among the leaders at least. The group still exists and meets regularly. I suspect I'm a thorn in their side. I have a big mouth and they've heard I give talks on reincarnation. Ironically, one or two of them got trapped listening to *my* lectures on reincarnation, at various group meeting.

Religious recruiting disturbs me. Not only the sales pitch, but the unbelievable arrogance in suggesting that their way is the *only* way. Also, the mindless fundamentalism they teach—in spite of all the available new information to enlighten us on spiritual matters.

The experience with Ginny was another negative experience connected with a die-hard religion, as far as I was concerned.

When You're Dead You're Dead

That's what I finally convinced myself while I was still an agnostic.

But one day, in the middle of a tennis game, my opponent Sandy said, "Pam, I just read the most amazing book about life after death.

"Oh really," said I, totally disinterested.

"Yeah," she continued, "it's got all kinds of evidence that there really *is* a life, just like ours here, after we die."

I shrugged and leaned over to pick up the ball, thinking, *"I don't even want to think about that again. I've made up my mind that death is the end... and I don't want to re-examine that topic. It gives me heartburn."*

What I hadn't counted on was that the subject stayed with me for days after that conversation. In retrospect, my previously held conclusions about death being the *end* weren't sitting as easily as they should have, in my mind.

Five years after that tennis game, I sat in front of Mary, hanging onto every word, as she told me I'd been a spiritual teacher in many past lives. Oddly enough, from the moment she made this surprising announcement, it felt right. And it still feels right.

Depression

My sympathy wraps its arm around anyone suffering from depression. I endured the problem for about four years in my thirties. There was no obvious *reason*. We had no particular financial worries; things were *always* a bit tight. The kids were doing reasonably well at school. My free-lance illustrating was going along okay. My husband's practice was steady.

But when I woke up in the morning, I wanted to roll over and cry. I had to leave an exercise class early, one day, because I felt weepy for no reason. I dragged myself through every activity, whether alone or in company. As the years went by, I went through the motions of living with a constant lump in my throat.

My husband and children weren't aware of how I felt. There was no reason to drag them down too.

Using armchair self-analysis of my problem, I concluded that I felt helpless and everything looked hopeless. No matter how much I tried, no area in my life seemed to improve. The kids weren't particularly excited by anything. I couldn't see my illustration business ever expanding because of the limited market. And so on.

Just as I was finally prepared to talk to a professional, the gloom began to lift. Gradually it disappeared. From then on, I'd accept things as they were, and appreciate what I had. I would stop trying to be a "Ms. Fix-it," and a super-achiever.

By the time I met Mary, I was relatively calm and content, about a "six out of ten" on the happiness scale. I hadn't gone with a problem, just curiosity.

But, from my first reading with her, where she talked about my past lives as if I already understood reincarnation, I felt better about *everything*.

At about the same time, I learned more about reincarnation and how it works from my friend Hilary, who had studied the concept. The explanation made such sense that something seemed to lift in me—from the bottom of my soul, so to speak.

The excitement and peace of mind I gained from this new knowledge increased with every book I read. The accumulating evidence carried me through seven years of financial difficulty and thirteen years of parental care. There was no recurrence of depression. Anxiety, yes—but no depression.

I attribute this calm acceptance to my growing understanding that everything is part of our soul's plan. Mary had predicted our seven years of financial hardship, therefore it *must* have been part of *our* life plan.

How we deal with our trials is what matters. And whatever we can't do in this life, we can do in another. Knowing this changed my life.

Marge Thompson, the next outstanding psychic I discuss, explained *why* I suffered four years of depression: "Pam, you were meant to go through that experience so you would not only be sympathetic to others in the same condition, but so you would take reincarnation more seriously than the average person—and would want to share your understanding. See how the spirit world works? You were depressed because you thought there was *no point in living*. Now you know that *there is a reason*."

Summing It All Up

Growing up in such a kaleidoscope of spiritual beliefs prepared me to consider *any* new ideas about faith. No set of rules fenced me in.

My late friend Jean (a Catholic) lost her faith for a few years and then regained it. During one of our regular debates about Catholicism, she admitted that "there are some things I don't agree with in the Church. But I've decided that if you're going to belong to a club, you have to abide by *all* the rules... not just some of them. I know it sounds funny in these times, but I've decided to go for it."

She wasn't kidding. When she planned her funeral, she arranged for three priests and an hour-and-a-half-long service to send her soul on its way.

I haven't found a club yet whose rules I'm prepared to obey. As my husband wryly attests, I've "always had a small problem with obedience."

I don't believe that the great mind that created all the systems and seasons of nature—as well as humans who have the ability to reason—intended that we should have to park our brains at the door of a religious institution in order to believe in a divine creator.

Pamela Evans

3
Marge

"I'll have to ask you to uncross your legs, dear," said Marge Thompson, the psychic who was facing me, both of us on kitchen chairs. I promptly uncrossed my legs, thinking the request must have something to do with energy flow. (Two years of reading about psychics and reincarnation had enlightened me, I thought naively.) Marge was an energetic grandmotherly type with a huge smile and hands that would be at home gutting a chicken or draped over the arm of a wingback chair.

In spite of her warm demeanor, the familiar chills accompanied this first reading. Out of thirty-plus psychics I was to sit with over the next twenty years, Marge and Mary were by far the most skilled and accurate. Eventually, my husband and I would become friends with Marge and visit her home on the Rouge River near Ottawa. But at that first moment, I was on the edge of my seat.

"I'll just ask you to start off by saying your name, dear, and I'll ask you to repeat it several times in the reading," she said. Ordinarily, I bristle when anybody calls me "dear," but Marge's friendliness disarmed me. "When you say your name," she explained, "I tune into your wavelength. The more energy you put into your voice, the more energy it gives me for the reading."

"Your guides are laughing around you," she said. "You've been looking over your shoulder a lot in the kitchen lately… it's because you're becoming more aware of them around you, they tell me."

I had been looking over my shoulder. One day I even wrote down "get a haircut" on the kitchen notepad, guessing that my hair was getting too long at the side of my face, making me think someone was coming into the kitchen when I moved my head.

"Watch out for your hands," she said, stroking her fingers. "You're doing something to them they don't like." This was February. In August, after a tense weekend with my mother-in-law, I had resorted to my nervous habit of pushing back my cuticles with my fingernails. The cuticles had become inflamed from a fungus condition that takes six months of treatment to heal.

"Your mother-in-law is going to surprise you," she continued." In May, three months later, she gave us money to buy a new car.

"I see you going east over the water," confirming the cruise on the St. Lawrence that Mary had predicted.

"Your mother will have trouble with a foot and a leg." She'd never had trouble like that before, but six weeks later she had shingles on her foot and leg.

"Try to see your mother's side of the story," said Marge. I did try, and eventually I had a more balanced view of my parents' marriage. (Marge continued to help me understand it even more, which eased my exasperation in dealing with them as they aged.)

Large and small facts followed: bits about past lives and other people, and a few predictions. I asked her if my late grandfather had hidden something, which Mary had suggested.

"He says [meaning Grandpa] 'ask the gambler in the family,'" said Marge.

The gambler was my Uncle Jack, who said, "No, I don't know of anything he might have hidden." Mary

Marge

must have confused the images of gold and diamonds that she saw in connection with his business as a jeweler, with Grandpa's habitual secrecy. (Most psychics do this occasionally. The other possibility is that I misunderstood what she said; with no tape to back up my memory of Mary's readings, it was hard to tell.)

Over coffee after the reading, Marge gave me details of her life. She was visiting friends here, she explained, whom she'd met in Montreal and, because she was a stranger here, was glad to chat with someone.

"I was born psychic, and so was my mother. When I was a little girl, I could see spirits of dead people around my friends. When I told them, they'd go home and tell their parents and then their parents wouldn't let them play with me anymore. So I was very lonely as a child. I just *love* my work, Pam, and the more readings I give, the more energy I get from them. It doesn't tire me at all. I love being able to help people with my gift if I can. Some days, I give fourteen or fifteen readings."

In her pantsuit and sensible shoes, she looked like someone who'd just baked a meatloaf instead of bringing messages from the spirit world. Her reputation extended to many parts of the country. (One day, a man from Calgary appeared at her door.)

"People drive up in the middle of the night expecting me to read for them right then—honestly, sometimes I wonder." Shaking her head with a bemused smile, she continued, "but I always try to help them if I can.

"My first husband played around with my sister for twelve years before I found out from my daughter. Psychics can't read for themselves, Pam, and we have to go through our own lessons too. Most of us have very hard lives, at least for the first part, because it helps us be more understanding of other people's problems."

A week later, I had another reading and took Dave along. I was afraid Marge might not come back and there was more I wanted to know. Dave was going to have a reading this time too. These first readings with Marge took place two years after Mary and Paul had left London. By now, I suspected that psychics of this caliber were rare.

She opened the door and with her big smile said, "Hi, it's Pam, isn't it? Come in, dear." She met Dave and introduced us to her friend, Diane. Dave followed Marge up the stairs for his reading while Diane and I chatted about Marge. I pumped Diane for Marge's accurate predictions.

"Lots of things she told me *have* happened," said Diane, "but some haven't."

The only way to deal with predictions, I thought, is to be patient. Marge was a psychic in demand, Diane confirmed. She traveled all over the States and Canada, staying with friends who had arranged reading appointments for her. (Hilary Alderson and I would eventually be among those friends.)

Marge and Dave came downstairs. My turn.

"Let's see," said Marge, facing me, but looking over my shoulder with her hands on her knees. "I don't know what we'll get that's different because it's so soon since you were here, but I'll try.

"I see a large party. You must go... you'll meet a contact there who can help you." Mary had told me about a contact, too. I wouldn't remember meeting any significant person until several years later. Although psychics are not good with the *time* of events, they can see seasons of the year or special times like birthdays or Christmas. The spirit world has no sense of "time" that we understand.

"I see a new area where you'll make money," she said. Another psychic as well as Mary had mentioned writing. But, as it turned out, it would be selling advertising for a new city magazine.

Marge

"New people, soul-mates, are coming into your life soon," she continued without a pause.

"I see a divorce... very unexpected by the wife... you must help her," said Marge emphatically.

"Make do with the shoes and clothes you have," she advised, "things will improve in a year." Actually, it took four years for things to get better—the time problem again. However, all the psychics I'd seen between Mary and Marge said more or less the same thing about an improvement in our financial situation. It happened eventually. When it did, it was sudden.

"Your next book will be on psychic matters," said Marge, looking at me for the first time. Mary had said, during my very first reading, that if I wrote a book about my *special knowledge* I'd make a lot of money. Right after that prediction I wrote a book, *How to Look Rich!* But I realized after the first rejection that it was metaphysical knowledge she'd meant.

Few psychics say as much in one reading as Marge, let alone in two readings in eight days. Marge is one of the best mediums I've experienced. She conveys messages from the spirit world as easily as she'd give you a cookie recipe. Experts make it look easy. Some mediums go through great contortions while giving a reading with half the accuracy of Marge's information. Marge herself used to go into a deep trance when she gave a reading but had to give this up a few years previously, because of a brain tumor.

"People think that, when a medium goes into a trance, they get information from a higher power," said Marge, "but that's not true. I can give just as good a reading when I'm not in trance. Besides, I like being conscious so I can enjoy the people that come to me for readings. I used to hate coming to, after a trance reading, and having people all excited about what I'd said, and I wouldn't know what they were talking about because I'd missed the whole thing."

Marge tossed out this bit of information casually, but I was sponging it up to tell my bridge club, who were the ungrateful recipients, sometimes, of these fascinating facts.

☙ ☙

She came back to London in May and gave readings on the third floor of Hilary's restaurant and cheese shop. My third reading with Marge was at ten o'clock on a sunny May morning.

"Hi, Marge," I said, climbing up the second flight of stairs.

She was leaning over the banister above and said, "I do remember you, but I can't remember your name. It's Pam, of course. You know, I see so many people every day that I just can't remember names, let alone readings, but some faces I remember. Yours I remember."

My back was to the sunlight pouring through the window, highlighting Marge while she chatted. Then, looking past me, she began the reading. I could ask questions while she was in this state because she could slip in and out of it easily. It didn't bother her at all, she explained. (Some psychics get totally disoriented if you interrupt them, or angry, or both.)

"Your work will get better very soon... by August or the fall," she said, "I see you in Toronto." This was the third psychic who'd told me this—and they were all wrong. (So far.) Three years later, I did get a new job in the fall, selling magazine advertising. It was the time problem again. She had confused time spent in Toronto during this new job with time spent there over the death of Dave's brother. The psychics had seen the two events going on simultaneously and concluded they were both connected with my new work. Even the best psychics have this problem, but when you consider what they are doing, it's pretty amazing that they get as much right as they do. The *good* ones, that is.

During that reading, Marge discussed personal problems in my family, for which I needed the kind of

Marge

insight she could give. I won't bore you with them, but she helped me to smooth out several knots in my life.

"Your guides are telling me that you've changed your diet to a lighter one. It will help you meditate." My diet had changed since I learned about my gallbladder problem. But meditation bores me; I had tried a couple of groups but felt like a bull in a china shop.

"By the way, your daughter is having a good time. She and her friend have met some boys they like and they're traveling with them now." I hadn't mentioned that Lisa was overseas on a three-month jaunt with Julie, a friend she'd known since grade two. Lisa was born to worry and had agonized about this trip, but her letter two weeks later confirmed what Marge said.

"I see you in a music and dance class in the fall," said Marge. This wasn't on my agenda; aerobic dance-fit classes have never appealed to me. But the following September I remembered the prediction as I dropped a check for a belly-dancing class in the mail.

"You'll be wearing a beautiful new coat this winter," said Marge. That prediction could be an interesting test of destiny versus free will, I thought. I could certainly use a new coat but I decided to do nothing about it just to see what would happen. In late August, while sketching some clothes for September newspaper advertisements, the manager and one of the sales staff urged me to try on some new fall coats while they were "specially priced" for an August promotion.

"No, thanks, I'm waiting for the January sales," I lied. "Besides, what I have in mind is a tough order."

"What are you looking for?" the manager asked.

"A slouchy reefer, double-breasted, two-button, big cuffs, long... to my ankles, big enough to go over a suit, and not black, brown or camel. I'm sick of black, and I can't wear browns at all."

The manager reached behind her to the coat rack, pulled out a red coat and said, "Try this one." I looked at it thinking, *"no, thanks"* ...looked back at the manager, put my arms in the sleeves and thought, this is going to spoil the test if I like it. However, I stared at myself in the mirror for about 30 seconds thinking that this was *just* what I wanted. As I turned sideways to check the "slouch" I heard myself saying, "I'll take it."

That was the end of the test—or was that the way I was meant to find the perfect coat for me? What would have happened if I hadn't gone into the store until after it was sold? I'm so fussy about clothes that the odds were low that I would find another coat with all the features I'd wanted. So, for the rest of the fall and winter and even the following coat season, I kept an eye peeled for a similar style. Nothing turned up even remotely appealing.

༺ ༻

Marge's readings were a hit in London among her clientele. Word of her amazing accuracy spread fast. Until now, Hilary had been her only booking agent, but I had so many phone calls from people wanting readings the next time she came to the city that Hilary asked if I'd like to share the job of making her reading appointments.

When we hadn't heard from Marge in several months, I called her to see when she'd be back.

"I haven't forgotten you, Pam, but my husband has a bad back and I just can't leave him. But don't give up on me, dear. By the way, Pam, don't eat seafood for ten days."

"Really?" I asked. I'd never had a problem with seafood. In fact, I had seafood chowder about three times a week for lunch at a nearby restaurant.

"I see danger with seafood around you in the next ten day period… so please be careful," she warned me again.

By now, when Marge said "don't," I didn't. Next morning, I found a note from Lisa on the kitchen table saying, "Mom, there's a seafood quiche in the fridge left over from a party at Anthony's," the seafood bistro

Marge

where she worked. The quiche must be the culprit, I thought, and filed it in the garbage. Thank you, Marge!

I *know* the quiche was the danger. "You should have had it tested," advised a friend. It really wasn't necessary even though it would have made a more convincing story for the many skeptics I argued with later.

There were too many highlights from her readings over the next few years to mention here, but I have to tell you about a few of the more impressive ones.

Jean

My first visit to Marge's home had a purpose: to drive Marge back to London in *her* car for two weeks of readings at the store. Marge lived about nine hours by train from London, just over the Quebec border, near a town called Hawkesbury. While driving to London along Highway 401, she turned to me and said, "Pam, do you have a friend named Jean who's in spirit?"

"Yes, she died two months ago."

"Was she a big girl and she used to have long black hair?"

"Yes."

"Well, she's here and she wants to tell you something. She wants to remind you of an evening at your house when she'd had too much to drink. She told you something about a mutual friend and asked you never to repeat it to a living soul. She wants you to know that she knows now you never did tell a living soul and she knows now you were a true friend."

"Boy, that's nice to hear," I said as I continued along the highway. "How is she doing?"

"Things are a mess at home. She's worried because one of her older daughters won't stay home."

Jean and I had been neighbors for years. She was "Mother Earth" with two sets of fraternal twin daughters and a son between the older and younger sets. Our lives had gone separate ways for years, partly because of a ten-year age difference, and partly because my working lifestyle didn't mesh with her "Helen homemaker" lifestyle. She thought my child-rearing skills left a lot to be desired and I knew she over-mothered her kids. But there was a philosophical dimension to our friendship that ran deep from the first day she moved across the street from our former house. I, as an agnostic, challenged her Roman Catholicism. We had a wonderful ongoing discussion for years about the merits of our views.

We had just got back together again on a fairly regular basis when she found out she had cancer of the lung, which in no time spread to her brain. She died three months after the first diagnosis.

Two weeks after Marge conveyed the messages from Jean, I bumped into Jean's friend and neighbor who lived across the street from Jean's kids and ex-husband who'd moved back home after she died.

"How are Jean's kids doing?" I asked.

"Things are a mess," said the friend. "Jennifer [one of the older daughters] just won't stay home!"

Polly

Marge thanked me for booking her appointments by giving our family readings on the Sunday between her two weeks in London. With only the four of us, she had enough time to give four more paid readings to my bridge group.

The first three had their readings and were properly impressed. But the memorable one was Polly's. She had been divorced from a doctor for seven years and had no romantic attachments although she had lots of friends. Coming into the living room after her reading where we were all chatting, she laughed and said, "You'll never guess what she told me. She said she saw me married and living in a country over the water

Marge

where there was a foreign flag flying over an American flag. My husband would have some connection with the United States. She said she saw palm trees and the climate would be like Florida but it was not in North America. And she said she saw me married or in a marriage-like situation three times in my life."

We laughed, discussed it, and moved on to other predictions. But I stored it at the back of my mind, being familiar with Marge's accuracy. The bridge group tended to take her readings less seriously than I, but "Truth is the daughter of time," as someone once said.

About three years later, Polly announced at bridge that her old flame, Ken, from university days, whom she'd thrown over for her ex-husband 35 years ago and who lived and worked in Italy, had separated from his long-term lover and was available. Did we think she should write him? "Of course," we said in unison, "what have you got to lose?"

Six months later, she was having dinner with two of her single friends. One of them, Helen, asked Polly if she'd written Ken.

"I've written a letter," said Polly, "but I haven't had the nerve to mail it."

Helen, knowing that she would never change her mind, said, "I think we should call him. Let's do it right now," and got up from the table.

Carole opened the phonebook, found his mother's number in London and dialed. His mother passed on his number with one warning: "Don't call him now, it's three in the morning there."

"Of course not, Mrs. Wrong," said Carole. "Thanks so much." She disconnected and immediately dialed the overseas number. After five rings Ken answered the phone.

"Is this Ken Wrong?" asked Carole. The answer was yes. "This is Carole Morris from London, Ontario. Do you remember Polly Potter?" Yes, again, this time with more interest. "Would you like to talk to her? She's right here."

Five months later, Polly was married to Ken and living in Naples, Italy. When the story got around about the prediction, I was bombarded with calls for readings with Marge the next time she came to London.

Ken, at our first meeting in London, said to me during a chat about the reading, "What if I hadn't been there to answer the phone when Carole called?"

"I believe now," I said, "that somehow the connection would have been made because it was meant to happen."

Because I'm so enthusiastic about the potential for insight from a good psychic reading, people often react to what I say with amusement. I'm getting used to it, but I can't stop trying to convince them of what they're missing. There's nothing to fear from *ethical* psychics because their purpose is to help people. But it's important to go to one that's been recommended by someone you know.

The Checkup

Dave and I drove to Marge's a year after the story about Jean. The weekend was not only filled with sightseeing along the Rouge River, but also with fascinating stories by Marge about things that had happened to her and readings she'd given that had had special repercussions. One in particular was about a woman from Montreal who came for a reading.

"You must take your little boy to the eye doctor," said Marge, "right away! If they don't find anything wrong, make them check him again. Don't leave the hospital until they find something."

The woman did take her boy to the eye doctor. After the first examination, they didn't find anything wrong. The woman insisted they check further. This time they found a tumor behind one of his eyes. The doctors were stunned. One of them told her if they hadn't found it so early, he would have lost his sight in that eye. The head doctor of the team asked her why she had insisted on even the first checkup since there hadn't been any symptoms. The woman told him about Marge. The following week, he went to Marge for a reading himself.

Faces in the Fire

One evening during that same visit, Marge said to her husband, "Sid, let's light the fire in the outdoor fireplace and show Pam and Dave the faces in the fire.

"I'll tell you when they appear and you be ready with the camera," said Marge to us. "You see, spirits love to visit fires because the flames can slow down their vibrations so they can be seen." (The spirit world functions in a frequency immediately above the range of frequencies we can see with our physical eyes. Marge has the heightened sensitivity to see that higher frequency.)

An hour later, we were sitting comfortably around the fire. Sid, Dave and I were looking at the flames, seeing nothing out of the ordinary. But Marge did. "There's one on the left, down low. Take a picture quick," she said. This went on until ten pictures were taken.

"I'll look at the pictures as soon as they're developed," said Marge, "and I'll mark a small 'X' near them to help you see the faces. Take a magnifying glass to the pictures to have a better look."

This may sound far-fetched, and I'm sure if my skeptical husband hadn't witnessed it, no one would believe. Ten days later the pictures arrived with a small "X" or two on each one. A small image of a woman in an old-fashioned black dress clearly appeared. Her deep V-neck dress, over a white blouse, had a long full skirt. She was holding a muff at her waist. I could only see three-quarters of her skirt.

Another image showed a three-quarter view of a woman's face with blond upswept hair and a high white circular collar. There were fourteen images altogether.

A Real Estate Deal

"You're going to be selling a house in Toronto soon," said Marge, during a reading at our house. "There will be two offers right away, the second offer will be higher than the first. I suggest you act on that second offer—don't wait for another one."

When my mother-in-law died the next June, we put her house on the market immediately. Dave's cousin was our agent and the housing market in Toronto was hot. This was 1989. Her house was in Rosedale, an expensive area in the center of town. An offer came in right away; we turned it down. The potential buyers came back with a higher offer, which we accepted. We signed the deal and made arrangements to empty the house.

By October 24, the closing date, the Toronto housing market had slid badly. Marge had prevented us from losing a substantial amount of money on the deal.

Another Real Estate Deal

Dave and I spent ten days in Pompano Beach, Florida, in April 1991. It was a last-minute trip—our planned trip to Europe had been cancelled because of the Gulf War. Looking at possible places to buy, we found a place we loved the second-last day. It was a wonderful set-up with about thirty villas, half of them on the beach side of Highway A1A and half on the other side.

An hour after finding the complex, we had a real estate agent show us through. There were two villas available, one on the beach side and a furnished one on the other side fronting on a private canal coming in from the waterway. We were only interested in the beach villa but looked through them both. The hurricane shutters were on both of them and that made it difficult to imagine the view.

Marge

We decided to think it over. I wasn't going to force the issue even though I knew Florida well enough to know how slim the chances were of finding something else that would suit us as well.

Three months later, Dave came home from a boat trip. His friends had discussed the price of cottages and boats during the sail. "You know," he said, "that place in Florida sounds pretty reasonable after hearing the guys talk."

"Can we make them an offer?"

We called the agent and made a very low offer that was turned down immediately. We made a second offer close to the asking price. But from the moment Dave hung up the phone, I started to feel uneasy. I knew the location and set-up was perfect for us, but something was wrong. I called my favorite local psychic, Eleanor Crawford, to see what was making me feel funny.

"I don't see any problem with the place," said Eleanor. "In fact, I see you having many years of happiness there. But if you do decide to buy it, don't wait too long."

I wondered why she said that since the real estate market in Florida was very slow at the time. But I still didn't feel calm or confident. There was only one more thing I could do: call Marge for a second opinion.

"Marge, we're looking at property at 11..."

"Don't buy it," she said. "There's going to be serious water damage, I can't say when, and it will cost you three times what you think to fix it up, Pam. They're [meaning her guides or mine] telling me... look on the other side.

"Do you mean the other side of Florida, Marge?" I asked, "or the other side of A1A?"

"I don't know, all I see is a crescent of water and small white houses. You'll be happier there. And don't waste any time if you do buy it."

Thinking about what she'd said, I realized she probably meant the other side of A1A.

We immediately called the agent in Florida, cancelled the verbal offer and arranged to have another look at the second villa that coming weekend. We signed a deal immediately that would close in November. The Canadian dollar rose to 89.2 against the American dollar in November, and stayed there for only three weeks during which time we closed the deal. We saved about $30,000.

Dealing With Death

"Pam, you're going to get a call from a hospital in Toronto saying your brother-in-law is very sick," Marge went on. "The call will come in the evening. I don't see him living a very long life after that. He's got a lot of health problems. He's been very lonely all his life. Maybe it's for the best."

Dave's older brother Tom was a dear soul. He'd never married and looked after their mother when she was widowed.

One evening a few months later, Dave was out playing bridge. His cousin Pete, a doctor in Toronto, called to say he had admitted Tom to Emergency at a Toronto hospital and was with him. Tom was going into surgery even though they didn't know what was wrong. He would call back as soon as he knew anything. He left his number and I called Dave. There was no further news until two hours later. Things didn't look good. The third call an hour later told us that Tom had died.

I feel his death was a huge release. I hadn't told Dave that Marge had said Tom wouldn't live very long, only that we'd get a call from a hospital. I strongly suspected she meant imminent death. But she wouldn't have told Dave or me straight out, because the news would have upset him and there was nothing he could do.

His life had been lonely and sad. He was a schoolteacher in downtown Toronto. When he died, the Toronto *Star* wrote a wonderful testimonial from his

Marge

fellow teachers and students saying how kind he was to everyone he knew.

☙ ❧

Marge picked up the phone herself – a rare event. For the next hour, we caught up on the four-year interval since my last phone reading.

"My work has changed, Pam. I've cut back for one thing because I've had times when I wasn't well. I'm not traveling as much either because I'm getting older and Sid gets lonely. And I don't give 'garbage' in my readings anymore. A woman came to me the other day and asked me if her husband was playing around. 'Go ask him yourself,' I said, 'I don't want to create trouble like that.'"

Marge can be a little blunt sometimes.

"I don't call myself a fortune-teller, either. Now I call myself a 'Psychic Consultant.'

"Last week, I was giving a woman a reading over the phone and I asked her why she was sitting on the floor. 'How did you know that?' she asked me. I told her I can read her just as easily as if she's sitting in front of me because I tune into her voice.

"I'm doing more phone readings now. Before, I'd give as many as twelve readings a day here at the house, and there was no let-up. People still come from all over the country and park in our driveway. Some of them expect a reading without an appointment— some people! Thank god I've got Sid to handle that part of it."

☙ ❧

As we were saying good-bye after her last trip to London, she said, "Pam, you're going to have three neighbors come to your door asking you to help them."

The first neighbor appeared at our front door in March of that year. She had just moved in across the street, and we hadn't met or seen each other until that moment. Tears streamed down her face as she stood there clutching her ample chest. She thought she was having a heart attack.

The second was our next-door neighbor, in her 70s, who called plaintively over the back fence, to say she'd fallen and might have broken her arm.

The third neighbor's problems took more time—several years, in fact. She too was a new neighbor. We'd known each other for years, but not well. Her emotional problems had two legitimate sources: marriage and the loss of a son. Now, she's happily married to a wonderful man she met on the Internet.

The parting statement Marge made at the end of our phone call was worth thinking about.

"Do you know, Pam, we've had more murders and suicides around here than we've ever had before—three since Christmas! I feel these [deaths] are people who took other lives in their own past lives."

4
Three Favorite Séances

The Index Card

About 30 people sat in rows in a fully lit room at the Ramada Inn, in London. My friend Jean and I sat on metal chairs facing Rosemary Keith, the medium, who was explaining the upcoming séance. Jean was the only friend I had who loved to investigate psychics and read books about related subjects. We'd both had many readings from various psychics that made for interesting comparisons. And we'd endured our friends' amused response whenever we discussed our flaky ideas. I was glad to have her there.

My mother had died a few months previously, and Dad had died just two weeks before the séance; I was looking forward to hearing from them. Jean had lost a young nephew in a car accident, and both her parents in recent years. She was trembling in anticipation of hearing from anyone from the "other side." The longer we waited for the séance to start, the more nervous she became.

※ ※

This wasn't my first experience of a séance. I'd previously attended several conducted by Margaret Needham, a respected local medium. Her slightly tacky basement room had held ten chairs including hers. At her request, we had sung (or hummed, in my case) a simple hymn, while the lights dimmed.

"The religious music raises the vibrations in the room," Margaret had explained, "And that makes it easier for my spirit guide to contact us."

Since the spirit world exists close to our vibrations, by singing, we close the gap a little, apparently.

When Margaret had slipped into a trance, I'd expected a whoosh of air, sparkling lights or *something* mysterious to happen—from all I'd heard about séances— as we sat in the red glow that remained. Several long minutes later, a lilting childlike voice issued a greeting from Margaret's mouth. "Twinkle" (her spirit messenger) welcomed us and explained the type of information he/she would convey. Predictions and spiritual advice came to each of us in turn. In spite of my skepticism, my messages eventually came true.

ଧ ଧ

The Universal Spiritualist Institute from Indiana was offering séances as part of a week-long seminar at the Ramada Inn. The contingent consisted of six mediums who taught various courses in reincarnation, numerology, astrology, the history of spiritualism and so on, as well as conducting séances and private readings.

Jean and I had signed up for everything we had time for.

"I need fifteen volunteers who would like to hear from someone on the other side [the spirit world]," the medium began.

Our hands shot up.

Opening a sealed package of 5-by-7 index cards, the medium showed the participants that the cards were blank on both sides.

"Please come to the front and sign your cards."

Placing the signed cards in a wicker basket, she added crayons and colored pencils. The lights

Three Favorite Séances

dimmed. ("Too much light interferes with spirit communication," an ethical psychic explained later.) While the medium closed her eyes to concentrate, a volunteer from the audience carried the basket slowly to the back of the room and then to the front again. Everyone had an opportunity to check the contents, if they wished. The volunteer placed the basket on a small table in full view of the audience.

While the audience was checking out the cards and crayons, an assistant covered the medium's eyes with an elastic bandage. Over the bandage, she placed a mask. She then placed a black silk cloth over the wicker basket.

We paid close attention while the medium concentrated. A feeling of nervous expectancy wafted over the room. It was the first time I'd attended a production where the audience was more nervous than the performers.

The lights dimmed, but we could see the basket at all times. No one moved in front of it. Silence was necessary for the transmission of messages, and the medium would let us know when the work was done. Ten minutes later, the volunteer lifted the silk cloth from the basket. Picking up the index cards, one by one, she read out the names.

I collected my card thinking, *"So far, I'm not impressed."*

Back at my seat, I looked at my card. My signature was still at the top-right corner. My name (not my signature), written in light purple (my favorite color), appeared in the top-left corner. "Merry Christmas," which had not been on the blank card I'd signed, was printed in red, over a red-and-green candy cane, which decorated the center of the card. (My parents had displayed two huge stovepipe candy canes at each side of our front door every Christmas for years.) "Love from the Perkins family," completed the greeting. (I had signed my card, "Pam Evans.")

"Too general," I thought at first. The writing *did* look like my mother's—sort of—but I wasn't sure. Then I looked at the signature more carefully— particularly the "s" in "Perkins". Checking it later against her recipe for oatmeal cookies and some documents she'd signed, I had to admit the "s"es were *identical*. My mother had an unusual swirl at the end of her "s"; the same swirl was on the index card.

Supposing the séance *was* a fraud, how could the organizers possibly produce my mother's handwriting?

Jean, always ready to spot a fraud, was convinced her card had her mother's handwriting, too.

I decided to reserve judgement until I'd taken some of the courses the group presented later that week.

Waiting for the rest to get their cards, Jean and I sat there quietly thinking. Was this physical evidence—the first we'd ever seen—authentic?

Years ago, when spiritualism was new to the West, mediums frequently summoned up physical evidence (apparitions, table rapping and so on). These physical demonstrations were necessary to convince people that there really is a spirit world around us.

"Because mediums are not licensed," she explained, "there have been, and still are, plenty of fakes. Look at the corrupt evangelists that TV has exposed recently."

The Apport

Rosemary (the medium) and two volunteers carefully sealed every crack in the room with wide tape to reassure us that no outside agent, or light, would influence the séance. This small box of a room convinced me that the upcoming séance could possibly be legitimate. It had no obvious hiding places for props.

The room and the small number of people present—by design—lessened the chances, in my opinion, of fraud. The tiny meeting room seemed

Three Favorite Séances

slightly claustrophobic, even after the two assistants left, and was getting warmer by the minute. Seven of us, including the medium, remained.

Rosemary introduced herself and explained the process we were about to experience. The séance would produce messages from the other side and apports from a loved one of our choice. Apports are solid objects that materialize at séances when the medium has the power to transport them—with her thoughts— from wherever they originate to the séance room. The process involves disassembling the atoms of an object telepathically, transporting them to the séance room, and reassembling them. Reports of witnessed séances, involving apports, appear in many books containing occult (hidden) knowledge. But I'd never seen it done and didn't know what to expect.

Rosemary asked us to check out the room and her possessions for anything hidden. We did. Everything seemed in order.

She asked one of us to turn out the lights and began the séance. Jean was beside me again and we both knew the other four people. The only stranger to us was the medium.

Two or three minutes passed before the first message came through for one of the sitters. I was starting to sweat by now, from both the temperature of the tiny room and the feeling of claustrophobia the room induced. Just thinking of the taped door made me slightly queasy.

The first three messages stunned and delighted their recipients. They were insignificant to the rest of us, but very poignant to the particular person.

Then it was my turn to be stunned. "Now, aren't you glad you waited for the money?" asked my mother through the medium.

My mother had suffered from Alzheimer's disease for years and hadn't known me for the last three years of her life. Nor could she talk. This message to me was the first coherent sentence from her in years. Even more surprising was her question. It couldn't have been *anyone* but her. Whenever I'd complained about being short of money from time to time— hoping she'd ante up—she'd say, "You'll always be glad you waited for the money."

Rosemary conveyed information from my mother about my parents' marriage—very similar to Marge's comments. I'd had a biased opinion of the less-than-perfect relationship and had blamed her unfairly, apparently, particularly when my dad had become terminally ill. Marge had said, "Try to see things more clearly."

When all the messages had been delivered, Rosemary asked her spirit guide to send an appropriate token to each of us with a message.

Silence.

By this time, I was certain—from my messages—the séance was genuine.

We waited.

A sudden clatter jolted the six of us upright in the dark. What sounded like small hard objects bounced on the small table across the room from where the medium sat—about twelve feet away. Lights came on at last. Six stones rested innocently on the table in the right-front corner of the room.

Rosemary rose from her chair—still in trance— walked over and picked them up. Rosemary seemed to know, psychically, which stone belonged to each person.

Handing me mine, she said, "This is from Nonie [my mother's name], to help you see things more clearly." It was a rough white crystal. As I accepted it, I thought, *"I hope this really is from you, Mom."*

This séance took place early in the week of classes given by the mediums. By week's end, I was confident that the readings I'd had were genuine, but not a hundred per cent certain about the apports. Although I've read about many séances that were hoaxes, I've never heard about one that was partly genuine and partly hoax. Three-quarters of this apport séance was genuine, I knew for sure.

The message that the medium gave me as she handed me the apport was identical to a message I'd previously received from Marge, but with the lights out I couldn't say I'd actually seen the apport itself materialize. I talked to Rosemary Keith later about my feeling. She sympathized and explained that the transmission of energy is so uncertain that they really have to have it as dark as possible. She said that once in a while the apports simply don't appear because of some sort of energy disruption.

By the time I'd attended that particular seminar, I'd probably sat with about 30 different psychics—not for a "psychic fix," but to explore the skills of each one and learn along the way. I had gained insight into my own strengths and weakness as well as my family's (probably the most important benefit of all). I had had two health problems pointed out and fixed them—after doctors had confirmed a diagnosis—with a drastic change of diet. Dave and I had bought a property and sold a property advantageously thanks to Marge's advice. And I'd been taught by two of the best mediums about the spirit world and about reincarnation.

Psychics aren't *necessarily* very spiritual in their own lives. They've developed their gifts over many lifetimes but they usually have other lessons to learn while they're here in this one. (As an example, Marge has had life-long problems with her personal relationships.)

Spiritual advice, if that's what you're seeking, should only come from a *reputable* trance medium. A medium's own conscious ideas, or her limitations, do not influence the information given in trance.

The Apparition

A year later, Ernest McNickle, of the same Indiana Spiritualist Institute, introduced himself to twelve of us in

the basement of the Spiritualist Church in London. He had become, by then, president of the Institute.
He explained his procedure for the upcoming séance and described what he hoped to accomplish. Each of us had registered using first names only. This séance was going to be unusual for anyone but regular séance attendees—or maybe Shirley MacLean. It was a "teaching" séance. The apparitions about to appear were not loved ones but spirits from the other side who would convey messages about spiritual matters in our lives. None of us attending that evening had ever been to this type of séance before. The occasional toe, including mine, tapped nervously.

Ernest sat in a small, square, black-curtained area at the front of the room. "Darkness is necessary for the ectoplasm to emanate from me," he explained. "Ectoplasm is a mysterious substance, usually white in color, that allows a spirit to slow down its vibration and become partially visible to humans. Spiritualists believe it is the materialization of the energy-body double we all have. It's this energy body—containing our mind/soul and spirit—that leaves the physical body at death and moves to the spirit world, while the physical body returns to the earth.

"The spirit world exists all around us," he explained, "but it vibrates at a frequency too high for humans to see."

The apparitions would appear outside the black curtain separating the medium from the twelve of us. The lights went down to a red glow. Apparitions, like stars, need the darkness to make them more visible. We sat in two rows of six.

"Holy Father, protect us from all things visible and invisible..." began the medium. This "prayer of protection" safeguarded us against negative energies that exist around us—spirits who don't know they're dead and want to talk to us, or elemental forces that can be harmful. When a medium goes into a trance and calls in spirits, he is opening himself up to unseen forces. Other situations, such as an Ouija board session or an alcohol-induced stupor, present similar opportunities for negative forces because conscious mental defenses are weakened.

Silence filled the room. Gradually, the first apparition appeared—a flickering translucent human form. (The apparitions' voices actually came from Ernest, but seemed to be part of the entities themselves. They sounded totally different from Ernest's voice and from each other.)

The spirit moved around the room in the vicinity of its particular pupil— as a teacher might— while conveying personal spiritual information.

One by one, we got our messages. The spirit teachers addressed us by our first names. And we responded as Ernest had instructed us to. Our verbal responses heightened the energy, apparently.

The séance audience was limited to twelve to ensure that the medium's energy could complete all the readings. Most mediums find séances draining after a certain length of time. The medium's spirit guide usually informs the audience when the medium is tired and it's time to end the communication.

I was so fascinated by each new apparition and message and the verbal confirmation that my friend Jean had to nudge me when my turn came.

"We are very proud of the work you are doing," said a tall thin translucent figure to me. "You have changed many people's thinking and expanded their universe. Keep doing the work and we will help you. The time is right for this information. Do not be afraid or discouraged. I must go now. I am Andrew Jackson Davis."

I had just finished reading a book about this famous medium who lived before the more recent, and more widely known, Edgar Cayce. Wrapping my arms around myself, I felt shivers and a lump in my throat at the same time. I appreciated having my years of effort to learn and teach acknowledged. And I wanted to believe in "otherworld" support.

Davis (1826-1910) was an American mystic, clairvoyant, and psychic healer who became known as the "Poughkeepsie Seer." Interested in clairvoyance and trance, he wrote extensively on the basis of his own clairvoyant visions. In due course, he became a leading figure in the American spiritualist movement.

Only Ernest recognized Andrew Jackson Davis' name, but knew nothing about me, or my teaching. The message meant nothing to the others.

No one else in the room had known who he was.

5
The Seminars

The Crystal Skull Seminar

Part One: The Skulls

"The famous Crystal Skull is coming to London, Pam," Hilary had said over the phone, "and you simply *must* see it. It's going to be on display at the Holiday Inn next Saturday.

"There's going to be a one-day seminar on the skull and related topics," she continued. "I can't make it, but I wanted to let you know. The brochure says that Anna Mitchell-Hedges, who found the skull, will be there too."

Reading the brochure while people gradually filled the room designated for the seminar, I learned that experts had carbon-dated the skull as a 27,000-year-old artifact. Anna Mitchell-Hedges and her late father found the skull in 1924 in Honduras during an archaeological dig. She owns the skull and has bequeathed it to the British Museum after her death. For the time being, the skull resides at her home in Brantford, Ontario—unless it's on tour.

According to the brochure, the skull was taken from Atlantis—before the final self-destruction of that mid-ocean continent about 10,000 years ago—to the Yucatan area. An Egyptologist would tell us more.

The buzz in the small ballroom grew. A woman settled into the chair beside me. The settling took some time. She removed her shoes and put on knit turquoise slippers. Next, she fished deep into her multicolored tote bag and drew out something wrapped in velvet. The unveiling revealed a clear piece of crystal. She uncrossed her feet, planted them flat on the floor, closed her eyes, took three deep breaths and offered the crystal to someone or something from upturned palms.

Trying not to stare, I waited for more.

Most metaphysical lectures I'd attended so far amused me as an aloofly critical observer. Usually, everyone else in the audience looked like they'd stepped off the third ring of Saturn. This audience—thanks to my new companion on the left—suggested the best entertainment yet. My bridge group would enjoy the report of her arrival.

London, a small city of 300,000, was a small *town* as far as specialized activities went. This remarkable event hadn't produced even one familiar face (somebody in the publicity committee must have dropped the ball... or someone at our local newspaper didn't think it was a worthy enough event to promote). In an audience of about 300, there were a few "argyle socks and sandals" among the Nike's, tailored pumps, and loafers—and some very long hair. But, overall, the audience looked well-groomed. I intentionally wore a "power suit" to these events to scare off anyone who might otherwise approach me to join a strange group. I was still new to the various metaphysical groups in town.

My neighbor finally reopened her eyes, turned to me, and said enthusiastically, "Hi, I'm Betty."

We chatted until six people approached the low stage. The elderly woman in the lead was Anna Mitchell-Hedges. Three security guards followed. The remaining two were the crystal lecturer, Carol, and the Egyptologist, Joe.

The Seminars

Microphone testing and last-minute onstage discussions occupied the next few minutes. Then Caroline—the first speaker—stumblingly introduced Anna Mitchell-Hedges. I learned later that just before the lecture was to start, Anna Mitchell-Hedges had been unhappy about the security arrangements for the skull. She'd wanted the room cleared for 15 minutes for a new plan. Apparently, she had the clout to back this up, and we all filed back out of the room while the preparations were made.

In the lounge, a publicity agent from Toronto—also in a power suit—informed me that there were people from all over the United States who'd come to see this rare appearance of the skull. I hadn't noticed *any* publicity in our local paper; here in our city was a fabulous artifact that was four times older than King Tut's treasures—and Londoners didn't know it.

"No process known to man today can duplicate the skull," reported the brochure I was still holding. The artifact is a life-size female skull made from a solid 50-pound quartz crystal. The jaw—a separate piece—swings in perfect balance. The skull emits flickering auric lights at times. And from time to time it creates sounds that have been recorded but never decoded. Sometimes the interior clouds up—then clears. No one has ever been able to prove or explain *anything* about it.

Eventually, it was time to return. At the front of the room, the sparkling skull now rested—silent and mysterious—on black velvet. Plexiglas encased it and three security guards stood close by. All eyes in the room were directed at the phenomenon. The room became absolutely still.

"The feeling among students of the skull," said Caroline, breaking the spell, "is that it's a data bank, which may eventually be decoded. But no one knows *how* yet."

Speculations on the skull's history and purpose followed over the next half-hour. "This one was probably brought to the Yucatan area from Atlantis," she said. "Several smaller skulls have surfaced, to date, as well. The Atlanteans had the necessary knowledge to program crystals to generate power. They could have encoded their ancient knowledge into crystal artifacts such as this skull. Researchers theorize that the Atlanteans had blown up their own continent by misusing this power."

Ten years after this lecture, I read more speculations in *Mysteries of the Crystal Skulls Revealed*. The researchers, who worked with the skull itself and wrote the book, felt that all the recently found skulls (the Mayan skull, the amethyst skull and so on) were linked up somehow. But the Mitchell-Hedges Skull was by far the most famous and performed with much greater results than the others. The images that appeared within the Mitchell-Hedges Skull were sharper, more distinct and vivid. The changes occurred very quickly, as though watching a movie. In the book, one psychic researcher reported a feeling of love, calm and peace around the skull. The researchers weren't able to reveal who is in charge of the activity or energies that they see in the skull. Their conclusion was that some very advanced beings having technology and wisdom beyond anything we know are responsible.

    Michael Kant, a well-known researcher in the Society of Crystal Skulls International, claimed that the Mitchell-Hedges Skull was created by the mind power of seven Atlantean Priests who somehow transformed the human skull of an Atlantean priestess named Shee-thee-tra into a crystal skull.

    The author feels that the time is right for the Crystal Skulls to be accepted in our society as repositories of inter-dimensional universal knowledge.

Concluding her lecture on the skull, Caroline announced, "The skull will be available for close inspection for the next 45 minutes. If you're interested, please come up one row at a time."

Observing a pigtailed young man meditate, cross-legged, in front of it for several minutes, palms upturned on his knees—I decided the process would take too long. I'd had a satisfactory look. So I left for lunch.

Part Two: Crystals

We reassembled at one o'clock. The skull and Anna Mitchell-Hedges were gone. The room was more relaxed.

Caroline asked for a volunteer for the second part of the program, to demonstrate crystal energy. Several hands went up. The chosen candidate was now approaching the stage. She asked the volunteer to stand on the left side of the stage while she positioned herself opposite her on the right. Caroline held two wire coat hangers side by side—with three fingers of one hand hooked around one end of both hangers—allowing the opposite ends to separate freely. The open ends faced the volunteer.

"Watch the hangers as I walk toward her," she said. Nothing happened until she was about three feet away when—with an even swing—the hangers spread apart at the free end.

The audience murmured its surprise and appreciation.

Knowing the audience might be skeptical, she asked for another volunteer from the audience to hold the coat hangers. The hangers repeated their previous motion at the same distance from the first volunteer.

"Try it yourselves when you get home," she said.

"Everyone has a field of electromagnetic energy around them, called an *aura*," Caroline explained. "It usually extends about three to four feet from the body. When I reached the edge of her aura, the hangers reacted as you saw. Now, watch what happens when our volunteer holds an ordinary white quartz crystal in her left hand." She handed the three-inch-long crystal to the volunteer and, again, crossed to the opposite side.

"I asked our volunteer to hold it in her *left* hand because the universal energy that flows through all of us comes in stronger through the left hand and, after it has flowed through the body, leaves from the right." She approached the volunteer again. This time the hangers opened about nine feet away from the volunteer—three times the distance.

Natural magic, I thought.

"The crystal generates three times more energy flow through the body when it's held this way," said Caroline. "It expands the aura by focusing the universal energy like a magnifying glass pinpoints sunlight to start fires. This is the principle behind crystal healing. If, for instance, you want to cure a headache, just hold a crystal in your left hand, and place your right hand where it hurts for about fifteen minutes or so while you're watching TV, or whatever. It should go away, or at least ease the pain—if the cause isn't serious."

(Later at home, I impressed Dave and the kids with my demonstration—which actually worked. I could see the possibility, too, of dazzling a few friends and skeptics, particularly those who'd majored in science, and *knew* metaphysical energies were "bunk.")

"A single quartz crystal sitting on a window sill in a room affects the energy flow of the whole room," said Caroline. And different colors increase different kinds of energies. "An amethyst crystal promotes spiritual vibrations, while green or blue quartz can calm down a classroom."

(Recently, I read that the Tor (hill) at Glastonbury was, according to tradition, a high place of the ancient sun worship and a circle of stones like a miniature Stonehenge once stood upon the crest. There was a special power in these standing stones with their metallic and quartz content. They provided a channel of energy, much like a tree, from heaven to Earth.)

Caroline reviewed a couple of points, and finished her lecture by introducing our next speaker, Joe.

Part Three: Ley Lines

Joe was a well-traveled lecturer on Egyptology. He'd written several books and conducted 15 tours to Egypt. He was a fervent speaker on his subject.

"The Earth has a system of energy lines," he began, speaking rapidly, "flowing like a giant grid through it. Some civilizations called them ley lines—the Chinese called them dragon lines. They form a dodecahedral [twelve-sided] pattern that underlies the whole of the Earth and can be considered God's acupuncture system for our planet. Like the meridians in the human body, the Earth ley lines contain subtle electrical currents that run through the Earth and are carried by land, water and air.

"An energy vortex is created at the various places where the currents meet or cross. It's on these power spots, that the ancient pagans [Druids, Celts] built their temples—known as the world's ancient sacred sites. Stonehenge, the Glastonbury Cathedral, and the Temple at Jerusalem are located on an intersection of these lines. In some parts of the world, mystical happenings take place near these high-energy sites. There is usually a well, a spring, or an underground river at the same location. In some parts of England, you can actually see the path of a ley line from a high elevation by noting a series of sacred buildings or monuments built along a certain line."

Joe discussed the endless stream of *other* unseen forces that influence us every day—love, hate, positive or negative thoughts of any kind that influence the giver and receiver, the effects of the Sun, Moon and planets, etc., as well as the energy from ley lines.

He believed, from his studies, that ancient Egyptians, who knew the higher laws of alchemy, built the great pyramids. "The huge stones were levitated into position and many of them were apported [atoms mentally disassembled and reassembled] from various parts of the country through the powers of the special people who possessed great mediumistic powers. And these same powers cut the stones by some form of laser.

"Once the mortal mind can accept the reality of these spiritual and superphysical forces and powers," he said, "the erection of these ancient monuments becomes easier to understand."

But the highlight of his presentation was a series of photographs of NASA photographs, which showed distinct pyramids on Mars. A friend of Joe's had sneaked a camera into the photo display room and snapped pictures of their blown-up pictures. NASA's pictures also depicted a gigantic face on Mars' surface that became clearer the closer we viewed the images.

"The original NASA photos have never been shown to the public," said Joe.

This lecture took place in 1984. As I'm writing this book, the only reports I've seen of these phenomena appear in two books, *The Monuments of Mars* by Richard C. Hoagland and *The Mars Mystery* by Graham Hancock. (Or the *National Enquirer*—a tabloid that *occasionally* reprints valid information, but whose information will never be taken seriously.) My point is that even after subsequent successful unmanned trips to Mars, NASA has *not* reported that these Mars monuments—clearly depicted in *their* photographs—exist. Why?

"Think of the implications those pyramids suggest!" I muttered to Betty as we gazed open-mouthed at the large blowup shots Joe indicated: "It certainly won't make the church officials very happy." Christianity likes to think that Earth is the only planet in the universe that supports human life. Maybe that's the reason for the secrecy. I admit that I had a shiver of delight at both thoughts, the pyramids on Mars and the reaction of the church if it ever became public. However, "*The truth will set you free*," someone once said.

"Many scholars believe," Joe said, switching to a different area of Egyptology, "both in metaphysics *and* science, that there are tablets of crystal buried throughout the Earth. These crystals contain ancient information far superior to ours. But these tablets will not be discovered until the time is right. This will be, they say, when the people who put them there—*in previous lifetimes*—find them in this life. The discoverers will know, intuitively, to study the information seriously and will work to decode it and pass it along."

I loved this kind of information and sat captivated through Joe's whole presentation. I now had a new area to investigate.

The Psychic Fair, and My First Past-Life Regression

We decided on the spur of the moment to visit a psychic fair being held downtown. Dave and the kids had heard it advertised on the radio that morning and thought it might be an adventure. The sunny June day begged us to get out and do something different.

The fair was located in a conference room at the Holiday Inn. The semi-partitioned booths allowed us to see the psychics giving readings, or waiting for customers. A pleasant buzz filled the room when we entered it—nobody we knew was there, but a crowd milled about. We agreed to split up and explore for an hour.

A young reporter approached me from our local paper. "Excuse me, I wondered if I could ask you a couple of questions?"

"Sure," I said, confidant that I could respond cleverly. (When will I *ever* learn?)

"Do you believe in all this?" she asked, indicating the room's activities.

"I believe in most of what I've explored so far," I said.

"Do you believe in reincarnation?"

"Yes, I do."

Then came the question I was half-hoping for: "Why isn't it in the Bible?"

"Reincarnation was in the Bible," I said, "and traces of it still remain. At the second Council of Constantinople in 553, the Christian Bishops decided that the concept of reincarnation was heresy. They excluded over twenty books from the present-day version that contained reincarnation passages."

"Was this the Catholic religion?" she asked.

"Only the Roman Catholic Church existed then," I said.

She asked a few more questions and we parted.

(The next morning's edition of the paper reorganized my remarks. *She blames the Catholic Church for removing reincarnation from the Bible, and for distorting the truth*, it blared for all my Catholic relatives to see. I spoke to the city editor. "Did you say it?" he asked. "In a different way," I replied. The paper kindly removed it from the evening edition when I explained my Catholic connection. I was lucky.)

After the interview, I noticed Dave in the nearest booth—eyes closed, head bowed and lips moving slowly—responding to the psychic's remarks. He used to make fun of hypnotism until he participated (for a laugh) in a shipboard hypnotist's performance. He had found himself lying rigidly over two chairs, one under his feet, the other under his head. Someone had actually sat on him while he remained stiff. He'd thought he was just going along with the act until the following day when a witness asked him if he was sore. He believes in hypnotism now.

Moving on to the next booth that advertised past lives without hypnosis, I asked the gentleman in the

The Seminars

booth about the procedure.

"Sit down and I'll give you a free demonstration," he said. "I don't believe in hypnosis," he added, "because you can see past lives without it. I'll show you how if you like."

"Okay," I said, sitting on the folding metal chair he'd indicated.

"Close your eyes and picture a door... any door," he directed. "Have you got a picture of one yet?"

"Yes."

"Okay. Now describe the surface of the door as you mentally move in closer to it."

"It's a wooden door," I said, "with inset panels."

"What's the wood like?"

"It's coarse grained... like oak... sort of medium brown."

"Which side of the door is the handle on?"

"The left side," I answered without hesitation.

"Now, reach for the handle and describe it."

"It's wrought iron... a curved bar... sort of a flat 'S' shape."

"Put your hand on the latch and slowly open the door," he said. "Then, as you step into the room, look down at your feet and describe the shoes you're wearing."

I saw long narrow men's feet in patent leather pumps with square silver buckles.

"Now, look at the floor around your feet. What's it like?"

"It's black and white tiles," I said. The room was large as it came into view, like a great hall in a castle with elevated stained glass windows, along the entire right hand wall.

"Are there any people in the room?" he asked.

I saw silent figures at the far end.

"Now, look up your body from your shoes and tell me what you're wearing," he said.

"I see tan stockings and dark brown knee breeches."

"Put your hand on your face and describe what you feel."

I complied. "I seem to have a narrow angular face...I think it's the face of a homosexual man who's an artist of some sort... working for the royal court."

"You're doing fine. Now, one more thing... hold your hand out in front of you and tell what you see... what rings, if any?"

I saw a long-fingered man's hand, with one plain ring on the fourth finger of the right hand.

This adventure had taken about five minutes. I didn't know whether to believe what I'd seen or not. But even today, 18 years later, I can still visualize what I saw that day—and clearly remember the large hall with stained-glass windows and the feeling of belonging there.

"You see," said my visualization guide, "You really don't have to be hypnotized to get a glimpse of a past life."

"How do I know it was mine," I asked, "or that what I saw wasn't my imagination?"

"I can't prove anything to you," he explained, "but if you use the procedure I've just shown you, by yourself, you'll be able to see other scenes the same way you saw that one. Trust your visualization, and do it step by step. If it feels right, it probably *is* real."

Later, at home, Dave told me about the *three lifetimes* he'd seen. In the first, he saw himself in a scene from the Civil War out West, holding a flag. In the second, he saw himself participating in a medieval feast while someone was testing his wine and became ill. In the third, he was polishing a blue crystal in one scene, and flying in an individual flying machine of some sort, in another—maybe in Atlantis, he thought.

"I felt like I was right in the middle of the battle," he said, describing the Civil War. "I could see the gray uniforms and almost smell the gunpowder."

The first and third lifetimes seemed very real to him, but he was suspicious of the medieval one because he felt he'd been guided to it. Incredibly, the psychic who'd conducted his regressions could see his past lives at the same time he did. She'd explained this before she'd begun the regression. In the medieval lifetime, she may have seen it *before* Dave.

Hypnosis, and "The Girl with the Blue Eyes"

Before I'd ever been regressed, I'd read several books about hypnotic regression. *The Search for the Girl with the Blue Eyes,* by Jess Stearn, was the first. Briefly, it concerns a hypnotic experiment conducted on a young woman in Orangeville, Ontario.

One evening, her father tried to hypnotize a friend. The friend didn't go into a trance, but his daughter did. When he realized what had happened, he asked his daughter to go back in time to a period around her fourth birthday. Her voice changed to a small child's, but she couldn't remember a birthday party. Later, her father and mother remembered she hadn't had a party that year. She was asked to go back farther, and suddenly her voice changed and she had a French accent.

"What's your name?" asked her father.

"Susan Ganier," replied the daughter. She said she lived in nearby Meaford, in the year 1890. She described her home, the location of some gravestones nearby, a well, and an orchard near her home. Her voice was deeper than her conscious voice and she was able to give specific details about her life in Meaford and about the inside of her home.

The experiment continued over many sessions. When the daughter's family and Jess Stearn started checking her information, they found the well, the orchard and the foundation of the house, beneath a tank range of a military base. They also found an old man in his 80s who remembered Susan Ganier and whose description of her was remarkably similar to the daughter's. Enough facts checked out to convince me, but few of my friends accepted the story.

Hypnosis is, of course, being used in medical centers and psychology departments all over the world to get to the bottom of patients' problems. Not only is it used to find the source of emotional problems they have which have no rational explanation in this life, but also to gain knowledge of patients' past lives. Once the patient sees where the problem started, the problem usually disappears quickly.

Two Past Lives: A Saturday Seminar

A few months after the Crystal Skull Seminar, Dave and I sat in a circle of about 30 chairs waiting for a past-life seminar to begin. As people arrived and chose their seats, I noticed a slightly familiar face. It was Betty, of the turquoise slippers, who'd sat beside me at the Crystal Skull seminar. She'd brought her husband. For the second time she sat beside me and we introduced our husbands.

Ken and Wendy Donabie-Dixon, who were conducting the seminar, were an internationally known deep-trance therapy team from Toronto. After they introduced themselves to the audience, Ken asked us to give our names and say what we hoped to get out of the seminar. He also asked us to describe our occupations, hobbies and interests in life.

"What would you like to have written on your tombstone?" Ken asked us out of the blue before we started the regression.

Mulling over this thought-provoking question, I decided I'd like my marker to say, "She made us laugh and she made us think." I sat back in my chair satisfied I'd made a good choice, and thinking, *"What a fascinating question."* Most of the planet's population had probably never pondered what they'd like to be remembered for.

The Seminars

"I've always been fascinated with North American Indians in the eastern states," said the first volunteer—a private investigator in this life. "I'd like to see if I experienced a lifetime as an Indian, and if so, what role I played. I think I was male in that life." (Research shows that we change sexes as well as roles in each lifetime.)

The variety of reasons for wanting to see various lifetimes was fascinating. Not only because I was born curious, but, because none of my friends are interested in past lives, I'd seldom discussed it with anyone but psychics—until this seminar. "Why would I want to know about past lives?" my friends would say if I mentioned the subject. "I'm having enough trouble with this one." Or, more frequently, "You're crazy."

But here was a group that was comfortable with their belief in past lives, and I was looking forward to talking to them.

Ken encouraged questions, and during the breaks I met five people who became acquaintances. My bridge group would finally get a break from my never-ending reports of new metaphysical facts I'd just learned; I now had another outlet.

Each of us told the rest of the group what period of history we'd like to explore and why. Two of us wanted to go back to Old Testament days. A few were curious about the French Revolution. Dave decided on the Battle of Trafalgar. Several wanted to try lifetimes in England, and one couple chose Indian lifetimes. One woman had always been curious about King Arthur and the Holy Grail.

Ken instructed us to close our eyes and relax our bodies from our toes up to our scalp, one section at a time. This was the first time I'd focused like this in a group and I felt self-conscious. However, I intended to try.

Ken was reassuring. "There's no right or wrong way to do this," he said. "Just try to relax. If your nose itches, scratch it, and if you feel like shifting around in your chair, go ahead."

Ten minutes or so passed and we were supposedly relaxed. I wasn't sure.

"Picture a meadow," said Ken, "any meadow at all. Smell the grass... feel the breeze... start walking across it."

I pictured two or three meadows and, because I couldn't stay focused on one, was afraid I might be left behind.

"Now, picture a hill ahead," said Ken. "You're going to walk up the hill... over the top and down the other side."

I scrambled to visualize and finally saw a hill.

"When you get over the hill, you'll see a large building. It's very old. Find the door and go in the building."

My building had no roof at first, just an old foundation. Then I pictured another more substantial one, but several images kept intruding.

"As you enter this large building, you realize it's a hall of records; it has all the information in the Universe and all the information about your past lives."

I couldn't get a clear image, but I saw a few boxes and shapes. Nothing specific—like in a dream.

"There's a door at the far end of the building," said Ken. "Walk past the records...out through the door... into a beautiful garden. Stop and smell the flowers... look closely at some of them. Now, walk out of the garden onto the grass. There's a path leading down a hill to the river. Find the path and slowly, there's no rush, start walking down it to the bank of the river."

I wondered if I was visualizing the scenes as clearly as I should.

"When you get to the river, there's a boat waiting for you. Picture any kind of boat you want...it doesn't matter how big. When you step into the boat, a warm mist will surround you. As the boat leaves the shore, the mist gets thicker and warmer. All you can see now is the boat. Experience this for a few minutes. Now, the boat has reached the far shore...when you step out of the

The Seminars

boat, look at your feet and notice what shoes you're wearing, if any. Then look at the ground immediately around your feet. Once you've had a good look, notice what you're wearing above your shoes. Examine the fabrics and note the colors you're wearing. By this time, you'll know what sex you are. Look a few feet ahead of you... there's a road running parallel to the river. Start toward the road. Notice the surface of it and the bushes and trees around you. Now move along the road as far as you can.

"If you can't see a specific image, just imagine one. The rest will follow... don't get anxious about what you see."

I saw thick sandals on my feet, and stones and gorse on the ground around me. My legs were bare—hairy and masculine. I was wearing a mid-thigh-length tunic. As I looked toward the road, another person appeared from the right, walking along it. I joined him and as we walked along the road together, I was aware of a soft-cover book of manuscripts in my right arm. I glimpsed part of a large city just around the bend to the right, but I couldn't get around the corner—as in a dream when I'm trying to get somewhere and can't. That was all I could see. The scene went black. We never did get around the bend in the road. One brief picture of an ancient city in the distance flashed again in my mind and then it was over.

"Now it's time to go back to the boat," said Ken. So we retraced the route that had delivered us to our various destinations—the only difference was that there was a gift waiting for each one in the Hall of Records, which we had apparently given ourselves as a souvenir. Mine was a pair of gold sandals.

Back in this reality, each person told his story. Some had a lot to describe while others had very little. "Each time you practice this technique on your own," said Ken, "you'll get more out of it. Now, let's break for lunch."

As Dave and I drove home for lunch and shared our stories, I wondered whether the scenes I'd seen were authentic.

I'd never pictured myself as a man in a tunic before, and I'd never imagined the scene where I was walking along a gravel path with a stranger, in any book I'd ever read.

"I didn't see as much as I did when I was hypnotized at the psychic fair," Dave said, "but I was definitely on a British ship with blood all over the decks. I think I'll try a medieval period for the next one, this afternoon."

The circle was happy and relaxed after lunch. Ken and Wendy began by telling us many uses for visualization.

I realized I'd been using visualization for years to enhance my wardrobe, and hadn't been aware of it. Being in the fashion business, as a fashion illustrator, meant that I had to dress like I knew what I was doing. And in my case, it meant doing it on a tight budget. So every fall, after researching the new looks, I mentally sketched the four or five new items I should buy for the season. Without fail, I would run into the identical item of clothing that I'd pictured in my head, without ever having to search the stores. It was uncanny. That is the essence of visualization as Ken explained it that day.

After his explanations, we settled in for another trip into the past. This time, Ken asked us to go back to a lifetime where we'd been successful by our own standards of success today. Everybody looked stumped. Nobody understood how to focus their thoughts.

Offering a few suggestions, Wendy started the relaxation and conducted the tour to the boat. This time I saw myself standing on an outdoor stage in an intersection of many streets in a medieval city. People were cheering at what I'd just said, and, when the applause quieted down, someone led me off the stage to my left. I was a well-known influential speaker in that life. (Speaking in public is something I really enjoy, which is not that common in the population. According to a recent Gallup poll, public speaking is our second-greatest fear—after death.)

I can recall the scenes I saw at this session easily. The question is whether or not the images I saw were ever a part of my life. I don't know for sure, but they sit in my memory very comfortably and feel like they *could* be part of my past.

Ken and Wendy concluded the afternoon session and we all stood and stretched.

As we formed a silent circle with arms around each other's waists (I feel very uncomfortable doing this sort of thing), Ken said he had a strong impression we'd met before as Druids. Who knows?

Seminars on Exorcism and Reincarnation

A year after the regressions, I attended two seminars at a nearby university with my friends Betty and Mary Lou who wanted to learn something new. The first lecture was on exorcism and the second on reincarnation (including a past-life regression). Having company was a pleasant change from going alone.

The first evening, we watched a video presentation of an exorcism by Professor Ian Currie from Toronto who wrote a fascinating book, *You Cannot Die*. Carol Davis, his psychic assistant, had in the video allowed the intrusive spirit in the exorcism to enter her body during the procedure.

This particular exorcism was intended to release the spirit of a young child who was unable to follow the usual postmortem route (moving through a tunnel toward a white light) to the next dimension after death. She'd become trapped as a haunting ghost (a spirit that constantly appears or makes itself known) in a home near Toronto. The haunting had been reported in the media.

The video showed Carol *personating* the child. She *became* the child in every way. She had invited the child's spirit into her own physical body, which allowed the child to answer Ian's questions, using Carol's vocal cords. Carol explained that she sends out a psychic signal to break the spirit's concentration, then focuses on drawing the spirit to her. The spirit uses Carol's mind and can then perceive Ian, who takes over the exorcism.

The audience was spellbound.

We were in a large amphitheater packed with people. The actual exorcism had taken about seven hours but the condensed video was about half an hour long, showing the most interesting parts. It was a successful exorcism—the haunting ceased after the procedure—but exhausting for Ian and Carol.

According to Ian Currie, ghosts perceive him as a teacher, doctor, minister, rabbi, taxman, investigator or Indian chief—whatever they need as an authority figure whose instructions would matter to them.

If the ghost has committed a sin, Ian will use liturgical language. For example, in Toronto a pillar of the Catholic Church had felt guilty about something when he died. He'd wanted to confess to someone that he had a secret wine cellar. He wouldn't leave the guilt behind when he died and, as a result, continued to haunt his home—trying to tell someone about it. This information emerged from the Bishop's spirit while he inhabited Carole's body during the exorcism. Ian explained to the spirit of the Bishop that he must leave the guilt behind and follow the "light" to be happier, and that he really hadn't hurt anyone. The spirit moved on and the haunting ended.

Carol added more information about ghosts in general. "They're not scary!" she emphasized. She's never had any trouble with them. "They might threaten you," she explained, "but they seldom do anything. Sometimes marks might appear on a person, as if they'd been hit, but they *will* go away." There's energy

The Seminars

around them that Carol can sense. "You *can* be hurt by someone who's *been taken over* by a dead person, but not the ghost itself.

"Haunting ghosts are trapped in a time warp, usually because they don't know they're dead, and they either don't want to leave their home or they want to tell somebody something, or get even with someone. A spirit, who knows he's dead and has followed the normal post mortem route, *is free to come and go,*" although, Carol added, "I've encountered some ghosts who weren't nice people.

"Being psychic may sound exciting," she says, "but I had a lot of opposition. I couldn't tell the difference between a person who was alive or dead. That got me into such trouble that I wouldn't speak to anyone unless someone spoke first. From the time I was eight or nine, I had to be careful whom I talked to. As I got older, I started to investigate for myself by going to the Spiritualist Church and séances, but people gave me a hard time.

"Demonic possession is rare, but it does exist," she continued. "Demonic possession takes place when a negative, unhappy soul causes trouble by invading the body of a person on Earth who is in a weakened state—caused by drugs, alcohol or illness.

"As for Ouija boards, they are not toys," she warned. "They've messed up a lot of people. When inexperienced people use them, they're sending out a beacon to all the spirits who are undeveloped souls, hanging around the Earth plane, waiting for a chance to come through. The Ouija board is just what they're looking for. They'll answer a few questions correctly at first. Then they'll get demanding. 'Someone will be hurt if you don't sit with the Ouija board tomorrow at 5:00,' they might say, for instance. Dr. Currie and I have treated many cases of troubled souls who've played with Ouija boards."

Carol prefers the dimension between lives (the spirit world) to ours here on Earth. "It's far more real. In the spirit world, we can't lie, cheat or pretend. Spirits report this state of existence to me from time to time. They say we make a place for ourselves over there by the way we live and treat others here in our physical lives.

"When I'm in a trance, the spirits *do* have hold of me, but I know what I'm doing... I know how far I can go."

"How do we know we're dead?" asked someone from the audience.

"If nobody answers you, you're dead... look for the light," she said. "And if you lose a loved one suddenly, talk to them and help them move on. If they weren't prepared to die, they may not know what's happened to them. And prolonged grieving holds them back."

(A good friend of mine, Lydia, was sitting alone in her apartment one evening, grieving for her friend who'd died recently. She had lived with and looked after the older woman for years, and she missed her greatly. Her friend had been interested in spiritual matters and had passed along some esoteric information to Lydia. Suddenly, there was a loud "thunk" from the late woman's bedroom. When Lydia went to look, she found the headboard of the bed on the floor. For this to happen, the headboard had to have lifted up and moved away from the wall to release itself from the large U-shaped hooks that had secured it. Lydia understood that it was her friend saying "goodbye" and telling her not to grieve for her anymore.)

Carol concluded her presentation with a story. "One morning, as I approached my place of work, a friend I hadn't seen for a while held the door open for me. We greeted each other and after a short chat, we parted. Later, when I remarked to someone how well my friend had looked—she'd not been well the last time I saw her—I was told that my friend was *dead!* That's how real some ghosts can look to me, as a psychic."

The Seminars

On day two of the seminar, Professor Currie lectured on reincarnation in the morning, and in the afternoon conducted a group hypnotic regression for anyone interested. The most memorable part of the morning lecture was his description of a private regression he'd conducted in his Toronto office.

"A young man came to me, as a last resort, with a serious case of insomnia," he began. "He'd tried everything the doctors had prescribed or suggested to help him sleep. He couldn't fall asleep in a building when there was another person in it. Under hypnosis, I suggested he go back to the source of the problem. He saw himself in a bedroom with beams on the ceiling, around the 1800s. While he was sleeping on his back, someone attacked him with a knife. The patient indicated a semicircle over his stomach with his right hand.

"'Now that you've seen the cause of your insomnia,' I said to the patient, 'are you willing to let the insomnia go?'

"'Yes,' he said.

"When he woke up, I asked him if he had any birthmarks.

"'Not any brown marks,' he said, 'but I was born with a curving silver line, like a scar, on my stomach.' And he pointed to the same area of his stomach that he'd indicated earlier."

The afternoon group regression began with about fifty volunteers stretched out on a gymnasium floor, each of us with our own makeshift pillows. Ian explained his method of relaxation. He then guided us down into an altered state by having us visualize ourselves as feathers drifting back and forth, slipping ever lower, until at some point we went through a tunnel and out through a row of trees indigenous to the country we'd chosen to visit.

Pamela Evans

My choice was Lebanon. When the row of trees appeared in my mind, they were not the tall cedars I'd expected. They were definitely poplars. (I asked my Lebanese friend Eddy, later, if poplars grew near the ocean in Lebanon. "Sure," he said.) Ian then asked a series of questions once he felt we'd arrived at our chosen destination.

I was a wealthy woman in a beautiful seaside home. My jade-green velvet dress with embroidered cream-colored panels of silk swished around my legs. (I'd expected to be wearing something more like a gossamer sari.) Breakfast was a syrupy fruit mixture of apricots and dates. Lunch was some sort of game meat with brown gravy (a combination I hate in this life). When I wanted to be alone, I retreated to a black-and-white tiled deck, surrounded by a balustrade, down by the sea. When I went shopping, I could see flapping rugs or blankets hanging from the upper stories of the shop buildings on every street.

One of the final questions Ian put to us was, "Imagine yourself on your death bed in that life. And see if you can see the people around you, if any."

I could see myself from above lying on top of the covers fully dressed. There were two women standing by the bed, but I couldn't tell who they were in this life. No husband was present. In fact, although I felt I was married, I didn't see my wealthy husband around the house or anywhere else.

The whole scenario surprised me. I've always felt I'd lived in that part of the world once I learned about reincarnation. And my appearance made me look as if I did. But I'd imagined different circumstances—tents, brightly colored breezy clothing, veils, lots of jingling jewelry, gorgeous dark men on horseback, etc. I constantly imagined myself leading a vibrant life in a Middle East setting. Instead, I saw myself living a very dull, dry existence in the midst of great wealth.

The overall feeling of that lifetime, when we discussed our experiences afterward, was of deep loneliness.

6
Astrology Explained a Lifelong Conflict

When Edmund Halley (known for discovering the comet that bears his name) scorned Sir Isaac Newton for his belief in astrology, Newton replied, "Sir, I have studied it, you have not."

Astrology is the science that explores the action of celestial bodies upon animate and inanimate objects—and their reactions to such influences. Astrology is not currently synonymous with astronomy and should not be judged with the same system of rational proofs as the natural sciences—but astrology does correspond to metaphysical (beyond the physical) laws.

An astrological chart can tell you:
- The finer nuances of character – It can indicate marked inclinations toward or against dope addiction, promiscuity, frigidity, homosexuality, multiple marriages, a disturbed childhood, alienation or neurotic attachments to relatives, hidden talents, career, and financial potential.
- Tendencies –There are no secrets from a good astrologer with the correct date, time, and place of your birth. Your tendency to honesty or dishonesty, cruelty, phobias, and psychic ability are there for that person to see.
- Susceptibility and immunity – We all have a weakness. Maybe it's a susceptibility to

accident or disease. Or we have secret attitudes toward drink, sex, work, religion, children, romance, etc., that would surprise anyone but your astrologer.

Astrology is not determinism (meaning fate or control by the stars). Free will is our greatest gift. As Shakespeare said, "The stars impel, they do not compel. We have the gift of free will to act as our conscience dictates or as we wish, in spite of our conscience."

Astrology started in Mesopotamia, now Iraq. (Two researchers, Von Daniken and Berlitz, think it started in Atlantis or Lemuria, a mythic lost continent in the Pacific.) Christianity eventually decided astrology was incompatible with its teachings because the church fathers mistakenly saw it as determinism.

The Renaissance brought greater tolerance and it eventually became fashionable to study astrology. In the 1850s, interest again revived in astrology and in the divinatory arts because rationalism didn't hold all (if any) of the answers. Therefore, men turned to the occult (hidden) sciences.

At the popular level, belief in astrology has never wavered.

Millions of people, though, confuse astrology with psychic and other occult methods of predicting the future. Psychic divination has human interpretation as its primary element. A psychic person foresees individual events, frequently only in part. Astrology is based on mathematical calculations and the existing conditions in the heavens (plus human interpretations). Astrology charts the road and reveals characteristics, but does not predict what will happen to the car and driver, only what *might*.

        ♌ ♍

Recent developments in science have shown scientific researchers that the occult may not be quite so far apart from science as it once seemed. A greater insight

Astrology Explained a Lifelong Conflict

into the nature of radiation helps scientists and laymen accept the possibility that radiation from outer space has significance to human beings.

Celestial bodies (the Sun, Moon, stars, and planets) affect us with a cosmic radiation that we can't see, from the moment we draw our first breath. Radiation is a steady stream of tiny particles hitting the human body. The human body is composed of atoms (with spaces between them) vibrating at a certain frequency. These particles freely intermingle and influence each other.

Radiation also influences the mind/soul component of each of us.

The amount of radiation and the duration of it is important, too. (Just like X-rays.) There are many different kinds of rays coming at us. What's important is the angle, the intensity, and the sources of the radiation.

The Moon is a dead body; it has no inner energy of its own. The Sun's rays pick up energy from the Moon's surface as they reflect to Earth. This is why a dark Moon has a different effect from a full Moon. (Ask anyone who cares for patients at a psychiatric hospital.)

♌ ♍

> "We are born at a given moment, in a given place, and we have, like the best wines, the qualities of the year and the season that witnessed our birth. Astrology claims no more than that."
> —Carl Jung

A Sun sign is a particular zone of the zodiac—Aries, Taurus, Gemini, etc.—in which the Sun was located at the moment you drew your first breath. An astrologer takes its exact position from a set of tables called an ephemeris, calculated by astronomers. My Sun sign is Aries. The Sun sign colors the personality so strongly that an amazingly accurate picture can be given of the individual who was born when it was, for example, shining through the constellation called Aries. These traits will continue for a person's entire lifetime. The Sun is the most important single consideration in a person's chart. An individual's Sun sign will be approximately 80% accurate, sometimes up to 90%. Isn't that better than no knowledge?

Because I was born on March 27, 1937, at 3 a.m., the Moon was in Libra. This means that Libra colors my emotional needs. Libra in my charts means that I need balance and harmony in my life to be happy.

The *ascendant* or *rising sign* on the eastern horizon is the most important consideration next to the Sun sign: My ascendant greatly modifies my personal appearance (the Sun sign affects it too). My rising sign is Capricorn, which means that though I have strong Aries characteristics (talk a lot and bang my head against brick walls), when I take on a job of any kind, I attack it with methodical organization. That is not a natural Aries trait. So, earthy Capricorn calms and balances fiery Aries in my chart.

My guru, Hilary, suggested having a natal chart drawn up by a friend of hers who was an "excellent astrologer." Dona, the astrologer, lived 1,500 miles away in Winnipeg, Manitoba. We had never met. All she needed was my date, place, and time of birth. The time was the only hitch; Dad thought it was "around midnight."

"Not accurate enough," said Hilary. "The zodiac [circle of constellations] moves four degrees every minute. So if your birth time is ten minutes out, you might be a different Sun-sign altogether and everything else on your chart would be incorrect, too. The medical records department in the hospital where you were born will have your time on file. And, for a fee, they'll find it for you. This information can also double for obtaining a passport, if you happen to need one."

Astrology Explained a Lifelong Conflict

Three months later, my natal chart arrived in a large brown envelope. *It is my soul on paper!* Parents, friends, and people in general have always misjudged me—so much so that I really didn't understand myself, and started to believe their opinions might be right. This chart indicates my strengths and weakness and the lessons I'm here to learn. It is so valuable to me that I keep a copy in my safety deposit box.

It discusses the inner part of me that a psychiatrist could never know about, because I wouldn't be able to supply the necessary information. Thirty years ago, during a four-year bout with a "walking wounded" depression, I could have benefited from this information as well as the information Mary, the psychic, gave me concerning my mother. That enlightenment, plus the understanding of reincarnation would have speeded up my recovery or prevented the depression in the first place. I now realize that this depression was based on (what I thought was) the meaninglessness of life.

Dona's interpretation of my natal chart begins with some insights into her philosophy:

"My approach to the chart, any chart, is pretty philosophical, something that you will particularly enjoy. I feel that the first moment of independent breathing, the first breath on this plane in this lifetime, signifies the kind of energy we are born with. There seems to be a synchronicity of the moment, so that an individual is born at the time and place, and to the family, that is right for him/her, for the soul's development.

"I feel that we each have a special place in the cosmic scheme of things, a unique set of potentials that is right for the world while we are in it. There is always the choice of flowing with the best or drifting with the most problematic of our potentials; the chart can show where these lie, and how to understand them as they are presented to us.

"Jacob Bohm, a sixteenth century philosopher [and shoemaker], said, 'Heaven is where thou standest.' I feel that that makes a lot of sense; for me it means that

I have everything I need to make heaven here and now, if I will only look around a little. And so, with a chart. Each person has been given innate strengths and weaknesses, talents and difficulties; he/she can make that unique makeup into something very special and productive, just given the desire to do so.

"One more philosophical quote, this one from Martin Buber, before we get into your chart: 'The free man believes in destiny and believes that it stands in need of him.'"

There are no secrets from an astrologer who has accurate information about you. The major conflict indicated on my chart is a lifelong clash between my ambitions and harmony in my life. Every time I had an opportunity to do a large assignment, somebody in the family got sick.

The first time was during my probation period at the London *Free Press* as its new staff illustrator. Just after I'd started the job, I'd had three wisdom teeth extracted that had become infected. As destiny would have it, I was assigned an extra tabloid that involved night work too. I spent that period in a haze of painkillers while trying to learn several new illustration techniques the paper required. I could have done a much better job without the pain and the drugs.

Four years later, a large catalogue assignment came my way. The day after I'd taken it on, Dave came down with a double ear infection. The kids were three and four at the time. Any mother knows the complications involved.

And on it went for several years, culminating with sick parents to care for over a thirteen-year period.

Once I understood that this was a pattern I'd chosen before I was born (according to the reincarnation books I'd read), I stopped feeling sorry for myself and easily made choices on behalf of harmony. What a difference it made to my contentment when I looked back. (However, lately, I have adjusted the balance in my life again. After my parents died and I

Astrology Explained a Lifelong Conflict

retired from freelancing, I had taken up golf with a vengeance and generally had a good time for about eight years. This past spring I started feeling discontented with such a perfect life and started this book.)
    The other big difference my chart made was in encouraging me to write and speak in public. This also reinforced Mary and Marge's predictions about speaking to large numbers of people. For the last 15 years, I've been either teaching a class in "unseen forces," lecturing on reincarnation to large and small groups, or doing interviews on psychics and reincarnation as the featured guest on radio and TV.

    I was puzzled when I first read in the chart about money self-deception, but later on it became clearer: *I had been sloppy with money.* I lost a significant amount on a dining room suite that I'd paid a fortune to have refinished and then sold to make room for an office. And I earned my black belt in shopping for a few years. I'm more vigilant about my finances now.

    My chart showed me who I am. No psychiatrist could have done what my chart did for me! How many of us really know ourselves, other than *what people tell us* from our actions or personality?

- "You're not normal." (My mother's statement whenever I mentioned a career instead of marriage or as well as.)
- "I don't know where we ever got her." (Same source, whenever I expressed an opinion in public.)
- "If Pam only worked harder, she would have done better." (My mother, announcing my failure to get an 87 out of 100 mark at a music festival, like my friend did. I only earned 85 for my solo. I was eight years old and had worked so hard and been so frightened that I'd lost weight preparing for it. And the two of us that same day had earned the highest marks ever given in the duo piano class.)

These and other misfired statements by friends and enemies alike made this chart all the more important to me. In fact, instead of a eulogy at my funeral, my astrology chart, minus the negatives, would do just fine.

Once I read Dave's characteristics in his natal chart, I truly appreciated how different they were from mine. For instance, whenever we played tennis together, he would walk methodically to the ball and pick it up. It used to drive me crazy. I always ran to get the ball so I wouldn't hold up the game. But Dave has so many methodical indications in his chart that I realize he was born that way, and I've learned over the years to accept his approach to life and appreciate the differences between us. (*Most* of the time.)

Everyone can profit from a study of the Sun signs, even without a natal chart. Linda Goodman, a professional astrologer, explains the benefits of knowing Sun signs in her book, *Linda Goodman's Sun Signs*. She says that knowing Sun signs is by far the quickest and most reliable way to analyze people. This knowledge helps us to understand human nature. .

You don't have to study astrology seriously to have fun with it and appreciate yourself, your family, and friends more. There are many good books (a few listed in the bibliography) on the subject that can help you get started. And you'll find yourself in good company:

- All British monarchs are crowned at a moment of time calculated by astrologers. They always have been and still are. Prince Charles will be crowned at an astrologically propitious time—calculated behind the scenes.
- Astrology is quite respectable in England even among the royalty, and used extensively in Europe, India, China, and the Arab world.
- Ronald Reagan believed in astrology for decades. When he became governor, he was sworn in at three minutes past midnight. As President, he insisted on a separate swearing-in

ceremony at precisely 11:57 a.m. the day before the official swearing-in.

- Lincoln, Roosevelt, George Washington, and many founding fathers of the United States were astrologers.
- Former Vice-President Nelson Rockefeller was a client of Linda Goodman, and J.P. Morgan wouldn't make a move on the stock market without advice from his astrologer, the famed Evangeline Adams, granddaughter of John Quincy Adams and great granddaughter of John Adams.

☊ ☋

Is life an accident? I don't think so anymore. When I think about all the predictions that have come true for my family, friends, and me, I see a plan. When I look outside at nature, I see another one in perfect balance, where nothing is wasted.

I've never known a production to take place without a producer, or a plan without a planner. There simply *has* to be a Divine Intelligence.

Pamela Evans

7
Life's Patterns

There have been three main patterns in my life.

1. My astrology chart indicated that the first pattern, a conflict between ambition and harmony, is a large part of my life

2. Audrey White, a local psychic, alerted me to the second pattern. "Whenever you need help," she said, "the very best people will be there. They'll be mostly men. They will appear because they owe you from past lives."

3. The third pattern involves two identical blind dates that were important.

Gathering ideas for this book, I thought back over my life when I found this prediction of Audrey's in my notes. Before I knew it, I had a list of thirteen events that verified what she'd said about that second pattern—and one about the third.

The Broken Leg

Something in my leg went *snap* as I pitched forward down the steps to the ice at the bottom. The skating rink was almost deserted in early morning. Nobody even looked at me, as I lay propped on my elbow, knowing I couldn't get up.

Suddenly, before I had a chance to be really frightened or get cold, a man came around the corner of the building by the wooden stairs that had caught the back of my skate. He asked if he could help, and carried me home—three blocks away. I must have weighed a ton, at five years of age.

What would have happened if he hadn't been there?

The History Exam

Failing my Canadian history exam was imminent. I'd skipped too many classes in order to socialize in the cafeteria. Having never failed an exam during 17 years of school, I was about to ruin my chances of graduating in May with my classmates, and suffer shame for the sacrifice that my parents had made to send me to university.

I'd borrowed the history notes all year from Don, a wonderfully eccentric classmate who loved history, and passed all the interim tests. But I couldn't absorb the last volume of work in time for the final exam.

A week after the last exam, my group of close friends decided to get the newspaper around midnight before our parents could see the posted results. For years after seeing my name in the graduating list that night, I wondered *how* I'd ever passed.

Years later, Don and I met on the street and caught up on each other's news.

"By the way," he said, regarding me with amusement, "did you ever find out how you passed history?"

"No."

"I was in the professor's office to get my exam results, and saw your paper with an 'F' on it. I lied to my favorite professor that your mother had been very sick and you hadn't had time to study or get to class very often. If I hadn't been such a teacher's pet, you'd still be taking that class."

Life's Patterns

The Job

Commercial art and advertising came first as job choices after graduation, and I'd squeezed a basic art course in between high school and university. But art jobs were non-existent in the city where I lived and nobody would hire me in the big cities of Toronto and Montreal (where I'd worked as a secretary) without previous experience.

A horrible (in my opinion) secretarial job offer was staring me in the face after three months of no luck hunting jobs in the art field. Three o'clock was the deadline to notify the law office of my acceptance. And pressure from my parents to pay rent was mounting.

Sitting in the kitchen in despair that day, thinking I'd be trapped in a secretarial job forever, the phone rang. It was Mr. Fenn, the manager of the advertising department at the local newspaper.

"I heard through the grapevine that you're looking for a commercial art job," he said. "Would you be interested in a job as our staff illustrator?"

That job changed my life, offering me the chance to build a portfolio so that when I left to get married I was able to free-lance for the next 27 years. It was a perfect way to work with children at home. No other art jobs in London turned up that could possibly have given me the all-round experience that that one did. For years I wondered what might have happened to me if that job hadn't come along. Now I know it was meant to be.

A Chance Meeting

Still, freelancing from home while living on about three hours of sleep a night nearly killed me.

"Sylvia, I'm thinking about throwing in the towel as far as my work is concerned. This second kid of mine has so many things wrong with him that I can't get any sleep."

We met, by chance, at a party in another city, five years after graduation. Sylvia was a known intellect and a published author by then, with no children.

"Before you do, Pam, there's a new book you might consider reading. In fact, you really *should* read it. It's called *The Feminine Mystique,* by Betty Friedan."

The fur-lined trap Friedan talked about was all around me. My mother was an alcoholic. Three of her friends had committed suicide and many others were power-drinkers. All of them appeared to lead fairly useless lives, which was fine if they were happy, but they whined about trivial things constantly and seemed generally discontented.

My "jobette" became a job. The advice from Sylvia kept me from throwing away the one skill I had at that time. Eventually, I found assignments in Toronto as well as London. What would have happened if I hadn't had that *chance* meeting?

Saved from Catastrophe

A few years later, I convened a huge production, "The Designer Showcase," for the local art gallery. This was to be the biggest fashion production ever held in London. It was a choreographed dance presentation by models from a production company in Toronto. A mile-long list of requirements (special carpeting, a special H-shaped ramp) kept me hopping over a six-week period. The downtown Holiday Inn ballroom was the location for the last event in a three-week Festival of the Arts to raise money for the gallery.

Two days before the show, I was checking out the progress of the nearly completed ramp at our local theatre, when a young man approached and asked what it was for. When I explained, he asked, "Who's doing the lighting?"

"I presume the troupe has its own lighting person," I said, thinking to myself, *gosh, I hope so!* They didn't mention anything about lighting in their written instructions (which I'd followed to the letter). I felt an uneasy chill.

"I'd be glad to do the lighting for you," he volunteered.

"Oh, *you* are responsible for the lighting," Toronto informed me when I called the committee. There had been absolutely *nothing* anywhere in the instructions about lighting.

My volunteer turned out to be the *best* lighting director at Theatre London.

By this time, 850 tickets had been sold. If he hadn't mentioned lighting, I wouldn't have done anything about it and the show would have been a disaster.

A Broken Foot

Sundance, our Irish setter, yanked me off my platform sandal in his haste to a pit-stop on the way home from a boat trip. I packed the resulting break in ice from the cooler and propped it up on the dashboard for the rest of the ride. Our doctor was unavailable, so we were at the mercy of whoever was on call in the emergency department of the hospital. My X-rays only seemed to confuse the residents that evening; they were discussing them just around the corner, in disagreement about what to do.

Then a new voice chimed in with a very different opinion that no one questioned. Dr. Peter Fowler, who had distinguished himself for years as an internationally recognized sports injury specialist and orthopedic surgeon, had come to the rescue. He'd just dropped by to visit a friend in the hospital.

"I haven't got privileges here, but I'll see what I can do," he said. Half an hour later, he'd put a cast on my foot and we were on our way home.

If ever my "guardian angel" was sitting over my shoulder, it was that day when Pete walked in.

The Newspaper Woman

Bonnie Cornell, one of Canada's top newspaperwomen, inspired me to write about my psychic experiences. We met through a mutual friend and had lunch several times. Bonnie had talked the Toronto *Star* newspaper into following a story they hadn't thought newsworthy, but she had recognized its appeal as a national event and was right. She was known to have a "sixth sense" about good stories.

"This information is right for the times," she insisted, when I answered her intelligent inquiries about my area of interest. "Why don't you write about 75 pages about your personal experiences? People can't argue with them."

When she read the result, she said, "Okay, now you can put this manuscript on the shelf until you get a publisher and, in the meantime, put a course of lectures together and see what happens."

What? I thought, I don't know enough to teach a course and I've never had any experience teaching. But I drew up a course outline and taught evening courses through one of our adult programs in the city. It was wonderful experience. I learned what brought a glaze to students' eyes and what made them sit up with interest.

Bonnie's credentials are what galvanized me into action. She died the following year. Once again, I was blessed with *lucky* timing. If she hadn't suggested the memoirs, I probably would have forgotten half the information I have in this book—and if she hadn't insisted on my teaching a course, I wouldn't have become comfortable speaking about these subjects in public. The experience led to talk radio shows, two television appearances (one was a two-hour interview) and eventually lectures on reincarnation, both public and private. Once again, the best person was there to help.

Life's Patterns

Dr. Cheung

Ten years ago, my health was shaky from years of various family stresses. My chronically plugged sinuses and my curiosity precipitated a decision to try acupuncture.

The first appointment was a shock: a total assessment of my health, not just pertaining to my sinuses as I'd expected. Dr. Cheung gathered information by taking my pulse the Chinese way (three fingers on each wrist for many seconds). After the pulse-taking, he wrote half a page of Chinese, then looked up and said, "Your immune system is very low. You are extremely tired. Your kidneys and bladder are weak—you must have to go to the bathroom a lot. [I did.] Your liver and gallbladder are overactive. Your circulation is very poor and your stress level is very high."

"How can you know all that just from taking my pulse?"

"It took me ten years to learn how, in China," he said. "I'll give you a brochure that explains the principles of acupuncture before you leave."

I agreed to the course of treatment he recommended. During the years of weekly appointments, he gradually explained the process, including the method of taking a pulse.

After the first three months of treatment, a close friend said, "You didn't go to the washroom either before or after lunch like you usually do. What happened?" Eventually the rest of my problems cleared up or at least improved 80%. I learned a tremendous amount from Dr. Cheung during the four years, and emerged not only with a new body, but a greater respect for it. He listed certain foods my body didn't like and recommended specific vitamins that my body needed.

Four years of treatments—three times a week—restored my health and rejuvenated me.

I also witnessed another patient's progress that was *outstanding*. Stan had started treatments around the same time as I did, in 1990. He'd had a stroke that had paralyzed his right side for the previous year. His doctors had told him there was nothing they could do. After four years of Dr. Cheung's treatment, he was out of his wheelchair and able to open a door with his previously paralyzed right hand.

Dr. Cheung was the vice-president of the World Acupuncture Association and president of the Canadian Acupuncture Association. Could I have found anyone better?

❦ ❦

As for the third pattern, even *I* saw it without being told.

Brian called me on a Wednesday evening in November of 1956.

"Hi, I'm Brian D," he said. "I met you in Bill D's car when he drove you down University Drive last week. I just wondered if you felt like going to Campbell's [our university's watering hole] for a drink Friday night?"

"Sure," I said. "Thanks very much." (We were more formal in those days)

He arrived on the appointed Friday evening in the rain wearing a navy blue trench coat. He was about 5' 10, brown hair, nice face, a deep voice and, as it turned out, possessed an irreverent sense of humor. I'd gone out with many guys in university because that was how we socialized then, but Brian was my *first* true love. He was the one who talked me into working in Montreal, where he lived, after graduation.

Over the summer, while I was teaching swimming at a girl's camp for the last time, he met another girl in Montreal. Our romance ended three days after I arrived in Montreal. Broken-hearted, I worked a few more months in Montreal before returning home to look for an art job.

Dave called me on a Wednesday evening in November of 1959.

"Hi, I'm Dave Evans. I'm a friend of Murray S's. I'm new in town and Murray gave me your name at dinner the other night."

I was probably the only one in Murray's "little black book" who was still available. We'd dated briefly.

"I wondered if you'd be interested in going out for a drink Friday night? I don't know the city very well but I hear Campbell's is OK."

"Thanks very much," I said. "That sounds great."

Dave arrived on a rainy Friday evening in a navy blue trench coat. He was about 5'10, brown hair, and a nice face. He had, and still has, a highly irreverent sense of humor.

On our third date at Campbell's, he said something that triggered a feeling of closeness that I can't explain. I *knew* that I would marry him if he were willing. Normally, in those days, couples decided to continue or end a relationship after three of four dates. We were married a year later.

Were those two blind dates *meant to be* or was I just imagining it? I now know in my heart that these meetings with Brian and Dave were no accident. Add to that Marge's comments that we were lovers in some past lives, brother and sister in another, and married many times in the past.

According to research, Dave's *triggering remark* that made me pay more serious attention to him was no accident either. All the facts converge to reassure me that we were *meant to be together* in this life.

Things Happen for A Reason

John Lennon once said that life is what happens while you're making other plans. The following stories illustrate definite *reasons* (in my opinion) for the frustrations and delays in the events listed below—and that the outcome was positive.

Pamela Evans

Lack Of Success in My Life

"Marge, why is it that I never became as successful as I'd hoped in the fashion business?"

"You were never meant to go past a certain point in that business," she replied. "You were allowed to make the money you needed at the time and to learn how to dress well, but when you weren't busy enough, you were forced to turn to other activities that involved communication skills. Those skills will make you a better teacher when the time comes. You came here to teach, Pam, and to deal with people."

That insight, along with the information about the conflict between work and harmony, showed me that my efforts had not been in vain. There was a reason for all the frustration over the years; I would get just so far in whatever area of fashion I was concentrating on at the time, and then someone's illness or a family situation would block me. Now I understand why. The thwarted efforts on my part directed me to learn new skills.

The Cancelled Trip

Our trip to Eastern Europe in the spring of 1991 was cancelled by the Gulf War. "Maybe that's a sign telling us to take a look at property to buy in Florida," I said to Dave.

"Well, let's go to Florida anyway," he replied.

I wanted to find a group of villas in Pompano Beach where I'd visited my grandparents in the '40s. We'd just inherited some money that would have been very easy to fritter away on fancy trips. So before we did something shortsighted with it, I thought that investing it in property (we could always sell) would be a better plan. We bought the place I talked about earlier. In the last eight years, there's been nothing on the market in our area that comes close to being as perfect as our villa is for us. The cancelled trip turned out for the best.

Four years ago, we invited Polly (of the Polly story) and her husband Ken to visit us in Florida. They

Life's Patterns

intended to drive down to see other parts of our area as well.

Meanwhile, Dave was waiting to have a suspicious lesion removed from his ankle. We had come home from Florida to look after this sometime in January. But there was a hitch. The hospital notified him seven or eight times that the operation was postponed. The endless delays meant that Polly and Ken's visit would be shifted to a later date, and that would interfere with their other travel plans.

Finally, Dave was admitted at the end of January. To his surprise, he was in the hospital not just overnight, but for a week. Then there were home visits.

"This delay *must* be for a reason," I said.

By the time we finally got away, Polly and Ken cancelled their plans to visit. There just wasn't enough time.

Polly called us the middle of February to say that Ken had had a seizure and been rushed to the hospital. He was having every kind of neurological test that existed before they booked him for surgery.

If Dave's ankle hadn't delayed their trip, Ken would have had his seizure either on the way down or while they were here. *That* was the reason for the delay.

❧ ❧

Think back over your own life or the lives of people close to you and try to spot the reason behind certain events that changed the course of their lives.

Ask people how they met their partners. You'll be surprised by some of the stories.

I'm encouraging you to notice patterns in your own life. Once you open your eyes to these patterns, you start to realize that, as Shakespeare wrote:

> There are more things in heaven and earth, Horatio,
> Than are dreamt of in your philosophy.
> (Hamlet, Act 1 Scene 5)

Pamela Evans

8
Palmistry

"You will have two great loves in your life."

"Really?" I answered reflexively to this entrancing news, from a strange woman who'd offered to read my palm at a ski resort. "How do you know that?"

"It's right here in your hand."

This prediction took place long before I'd ever been to a psychic. And now that I'm in my sixties, it looks like she was right.

My goal in learning palmistry was to see if it was a genuine metaphysical science. In other words—to see if it really worked and, if so, whether if would provide me with new information about myself—and possibly, others.

After reading the palms of some friends, whom I failed to convince—because I knew them too well, they argued—I realized I'd never believe in palmistry unless I tried it on strangers. My uncle's funeral provided the opportunity. Once I'd read one palm, people started to gather around. What a hit I'd have been at fraternity parties if I'd had the skill then! These new volunteers and I were both surprised when I told them facts about their character they could confirm.

I'd never before met these people whose palms I was reading. But with my new skill, I was able to tell them a surprising number of details about themselves. For instance, the number of significant loves they would have in this life. Or whether they were intuitive or methodical thinkers. If they were an extrovert or introvert. Or possessed flexible or rigid personalities. I knew if they were a nervous personality or if they'd had a stressful event in the last three months.

The only scary part was seeing a serious illness, if there was one, in the past, present, or future. I'd never discuss a future illness, but a few times I'd mention a past one just to test my ability (or show off). I was right often enough to convince myself that the practice of genuine palmistry is real—though there *are* fakes around.

A person doesn't have to be psychic to learn it. *I'm not psychic*. However, Mary warned me not to do it for others. She explained that it's safer to be psychic if you're going to read other people's palms. Sometimes, the lines get confusing and people might try to read between my words and get frightened, or worry about what I *wasn't* saying.

But in everyday life I use it all the time (because I'm nosy) to get clues to a friend's or an acquaintance's character. One day during a dental visit, having just noticed his flat fingernails (indicating he's an introvert), I said to my dentist who was also a friend, "Jack, did you know you're really an introvert at heart?" We'd been chatting intermittently between spits and taking impressions about golf. Until that observation, I'd known him mainly from party chats and dental visits. He paused, hands and instruments hovering in mid-air over my face, and said, "Hmm; maybe that's why I'd rather be alone when I get home from work. I'd always thought it was because I'd been with people all day. But now that you mention it, I think I probably am."

At my next appointment he said, "I asked Sandy [his wife] if she thought I was an introvert and she said, 'Definitely.'"

Not only is palmistry a new tool for self-knowledge, but it's fun to get secret insight on other people. And the ability to read hands can be helpful in life. If, for instance, you're interviewing a person for a sales job, and realize from looking at the back of the applicant's hands (the back of the hand and the nails indicate a person's general characteristics) that he or she is really an introvert rather than the necessary extrovert, you might select a different candidate.

Theories of How Palmistry Works

One of the most complete books I've read, *The Practice of Palmistry*, by C. de Saint-Germain, explained that the lines form on a baby's palms the moment it takes its first breath. At that moment, universal energy enters the body to start its pattern of destiny, which the soul of the baby has prearranged (with the help of loving entities in the spirit world) before its birth. This energy enters the body primarily through the hands and feet, and starts a constant energy cycle through the body to the brain and out again. The lines themselves, formed by this electrical energy, vanish if the nerves between the brain and palm are severed. They will reappear once the nerves are reconnected. The subconscious, which knows the history of the soul's lives as well as the future the soul has chosen, forms the lines.

The lines in the left hand show the pattern of destiny as well as talents and weaknesses brought through from other lives. The right hand indicates the way a person has coped with what he/she has chosen to experience. For instance, if a person's left hand has a ragged heart line, it shows either a weak circulatory system, or a series of emotional upsets. These are destined to be in effect throughout a person's life. The right hand may show, by a cleaner, straighter line, that the person has either coped well with the upsets, or has looked after his health intelligently.

A baby's palm can be read just as easily as that of an adult. Age has nothing to do with the number of destiny lines. However, a nervous personality will have a very lined palm, from all the excess energy. The lines, formed at birth, indicate the soul's destiny and only the emotion resulting from life's events—as they happen—may change some of them. Medical science is starting to investigate seriously the connection between signs found on the palms and nails with conditions in the body.

If the lines on the palm form when a baby takes its first breath, and if a person's astrological chart is calculated from that same event, is that the moment when the soul joins the body? Edgar Cayce stated in trance readings that a person's soul usually enters the body shortly before birth, sometimes at the moment of birth, and sometimes days or a week after birth. My argument about abortion is based on this information: If a soul comes from another place and leaves the body at death to go to back to that place, then *nothing* can destroy it. It is eternal. All religions agree on that point. Elizabeth Kübler-Ross once said in an interview, "Would a soul which is part of God enter a fetus when it knew the fetus would be destroyed?" To believe so, in my opinion, would insult the intelligence of God.

A Few More Interesting Points about Hands

The hand is the organ of organs. Aristotle wrote, "Lines have not been traced without cause in the hands of men. They evidently emanate from the influence of heaven and from human individuality." Every element in the body is combined to form distinct individuality: our faces, our skulls, the length of our legs, our bearing, looks, gestures—above all, the hand.

The hand betrays the idea of mystery, recklessness, strength, laziness, even repulsion and mental illness.

The sense of touch is the most indispensable of the five senses.

Lines are just as clear in idle society women as in people who work with their hands.

A paralyzed hand will have no lines while the other hand on the same person will.

The major lines are present at birth (showing character and some major events). Minor lines develop later (showing personality, talents, drawbacks, achievements, and shortcomings).

No racial characteristics appear in hands. Hand characteristics are the same anywhere.

Health matters, past and future are marked on the lines, too, both physical and emotional.

Future events cast shadows ahead. The subconscious knows the future.

It's not possible to tell precise times from the lines in a hand.

Having Fun with Palmistry

I hope the previous facts I discussed about hands will heighten your appreciation of unseen forces working around us and how our bodies—especially our hands—reveal some truth about our souls to those who are willing to learn.

Apart from that, if you're willing to spend a few hours reading one of the many available books on palmistry, you will open your mind to another tool (along with astrology, numerology, graphology, and so on) to enlighten yourself about you. The more we know ourselves, the better we may deal with our lessons. And, even if you only want to learn a bit about palmistry, you can learn enough about other people—just by glancing at their hands—to have *some* instant insight.

For instance:

- When someone is facing me while holding a telephone to his ear, I can see from the short lines below his baby finger how many loves (not necessarily marriages) he's had or will have.

- If someone has a white spot on a fingernail, or several spots, I know they've had a worry or stressful situation within the last three months.

- If someone has very convex fingernails—from side to side—I know without any doubt that he's an extrovert. Conversely, flat nails indicate he's an introvert.

- If a person has puffy pads on his fingers, close to the palm on the inside of the hand, it usually means that they have excess appetites. This will show even on people who aren't necessarily plump.

- When a person gestures while talking, I can see signs of mental disturbance from certain movements. In one case, an acquaintance now has Alzheimer's disease, and in another, the person I noticed is unbelievably childish for a grown woman.

- If a person constantly points his finger at me while speaking, not only does it make me uncomfortable, but I know that the person wants to take charge of the conversation.

- In a meeting (if everyone is sitting at a table), a person who's intermittently tapping the table with his index finger wants to take control of the meeting.

- The longer a person's thumbs are, the more intelligent he is likely to be. Just think how short an ape's thumbs are.

- Rarely, a person has a shorter bulbous thumb called a "murderer's thumb." This bulb at the end of the thumb indicates extraordinary energy in that person. It doesn't mean that the person is a murderer, but it does mean that whatever they do, they do it with more energy

Palmistry

than the average bear. So if they get mad or are irrational, stand back!

If you're as curious about people as I am, you'll find yourself noticing people's hands more and more once you know what to look for. If you also know the general characteristics of Sun signs *and* you know a person's birthday, you'll now have three new tools to give you the kind of instant insight that a person's close friends take years to learn.

By learning palmistry, you'll have opened a new door to the unseen world around you and know that hands are another window to the soul.

Pamela Evans

9
My Reincarnation Experiences

The Silver Ball

"Pammer, get up on the chair and put your hand on the silver ball—I want to take your picture," said my beloved grandfather, using his nickname for me.

"I don't want to, Grandpa."

His tone of voice was pleasant, but something in his request triggered a totally unreasonable "out of character" reply from me.

We were in the beautifully manicured sunken garden beside his home one sunny morning. It was grandpa's pride and joy. A large fishpond at one end, surrounded by exotic grasses, set off round, oblong, and diamond-shaped gardens in the center. The silver ball in question was near the back on a cement pedestal. Flowering lilacs, apple trees, and stately pyramidal oaks guarded the geometrically planted blooms.

"Don't be silly, just put your hand on the ball," he repeated in a reasonable tone.

Suddenly, a ballooning rage started from the bottom of my socks. He didn't care how I felt about his instructions—the first person I'd ever adored was betraying me. My three-and-a-half-year-old body was rigid and a series of screeching protests exploded out of my mouth, aimed at this wonderful person everyone loved.

My hands were clenched at the sides of my red-and-white striped smock dress. Looking straight ahead, I was aware that Dad had come down from the side porch above us. The rest of the family (I learned later) was leaning over the balustrade to see what the racket was. No one had ever raised a voice in anger at a family gathering, it seems.

Dad murmured something to Grandpa and then very quietly reasoned with me. A resulting photo showed two dark eyes smoldering with rage, framed by a black ball of frizzy hair, staring straight at the camera over a silver ball held down by a pudgy hand.

Although I was an only child and the first of 11 grandchildren, my parents didn't spoil me. Good behavior and manners were strictly enforced if I wanted to be with adults or go to nice restaurants. Even my mother admitted I was a good child.

This rage came from another place and time. I now feel it was some final balancing of unfinished business with my grandfather from a previous lifetime. That confrontation might have taught him never to try to control me again, in any lifetime. It did teach me to speak up if I felt I was being treated unfairly. Once I finally got over the hurt that my perception of his attitude created (it took a long time), there was never another incident even close to it. And never again did I raise my voice in anger to another person.

Ali Baba

The movie *Ali Baba and the 40 Thieves* terrified me. Sitting with my parents at the theatre, a reasonably calm five-year-old, I started feeling uneasy soon after it started. But the moment Ali Baba and his thieves trotted on horseback into a cave on the left side of the movie screen, I started to sob and hid my head in my lap. I panicked and begged to go home.

Both my parents and I were surprised by my outburst. All the previous movies I'd seen had been fascinating. I remember feeling guilty, as we walked home, that they'd spent money on the tickets and didn't get to see the show.

Only after learning about past lives did I remember that episode and attribute it to a possible unhappy past-life experience connected with a cave and clothing similar to the costumes in the movie. Years later, a psychic described a past life of mine as a Persian, who, while fighting on horseback, sliced open an opponent's throat. Maybe that was the lifetime I subconsciously remembered at the movie. Even if it wasn't, I hope I've already paid off *that* karma.

Wine Velvet

One day, I was sitting in front of an oval mirror in my bedroom admiring myself draped in a remnant of cranberry-colored velvet from a box of old costumes in our basement. My mother's long pearls hung straight down my seven-year-old chest. Sitting sideways to the mirror and looking at myself over my shoulder, I suddenly *saw myself as a woman (in my mind's eye) sitting at a long table with other men and women*. The setting, in retrospect, was a medieval feast. Torches illuminated the walls and candelabra cast a romantic glow over the wineglasses and platters of food. In that tableau, I was wearing an off-the-shoulder gown of deep red velvet and had long *smooth* black hair. My hair, at age seven, was a black frizzy mop.

Subconscious Fragments

The hair on my arms has risen many times through the years around specific types of scenery. Late-afternoon sun shining through a row of trees will do it. Or shining through trees around a small pond. Certain misty summer mornings near large trees affect me, too. But only those two times of the day create that magic for me.

A researcher suggests that memories created by some scenery (also certain names of people, places, or music) bypass our conscious minds and affect our physical bodies, with goose bumps, unexpected rages, tears of happiness or sadness, etc.

Family Connection

One afternoon, Dave and I were reading in our family room. Glancing at him through the blur of my new reading glasses, I suddenly noticed a "my-side-of-the-family" look about his face. Past lives were not part of my vocabulary at that time. He'd never looked like he belonged to the Evans family. In fact, he'd been the butt of many a family joke about that fact. That day, I realized he looked like he belonged to mine. I began to wonder about a much deeper connection that I couldn't explain.

Many years later, Marge told me, "You and Dave have been friends, lovers, and married in past lives, but not too long ago you were brother and sister, too." That may be an explanation for our slight physical similarity. If you visualize Ethel and Bobby Kennedy, particularly the shape of their mouths and teeth, you'll probably notice their similarity to each other. Once you're aware of this, you'll notice it often in other couples, particularly in wedding or engagement pictures.

Past Lives and the Church

The institution of Catholicism made me uneasy for as long as I can remember. Now that I have the knowledge from psychics that I was boiled in oil and burned at the stake for being a thorn in the Church's side (spiritually speaking) in past lives, the uneasiness makes sense.

At Halloween one year, my cousin John appeared unexpectedly at the door dressed in an all-black costume revealing only his face. In my mind's eye, I saw flames shooting up behind him and instantly sensed that I'd been on the losing side of the Inquisition. A psychic told me later that I'd made the priests jealous in a past life. The church's dim view of my teachings had led to various forms of persecution. It appears I have every reason to feel the way I do.

A Three-Way Friendship from Another Life

When I asked a deep-trance psychic why I felt discomfort about Catholicism, he described a lifetime as a nun in Lyons, France, in the 1600s. "Your family," he said, "had talked you into entering the convent. I see you gazing longingly over the convent walls, at the thatched roofs of houses, wishing you were free to marry and have a family. You died of cancer of the stomach [from resentment] at age 52. There were two friends looking after you in that life, that you know in this one."

When I mentioned this to my late friend Jean (the friend who sent me a message in the car through Marge), she said, "Oh my god, Bonnie Hopkins [a local psychic] said that I was a Mother Superior in a convent in France in the 1600s. She said that I have two friends in this life, who were close friends then. I always knew one was my friend Shelley, but I never realized the other one was *you*."

Four Psychics, Same Name

Over the last 20 years, *four* different psychics (from different places) described my past life about 2,000 years ago as a Jewish woman around the time of Jesus. Two of them said my name was Miriam (a common name then), but two psychics also said my sister's name was Bethel.

Other Glimpses: Jewish Past Lives

Bonnie, a local psychic, said, "If I remember one thing about this first reading for you, Pam, it will be the number of Jewish lifetimes you've had, both as a man and a woman."

My job as a fashion illustrator introduced me to many Jewish clients both here and in Toronto. Some of them became friends and invited us to large parties at their homes. After we got to know each other better, some of them said I looked more Jewish than they did.

My Son, My Teacher

Years ago, a visiting psychic said, "Your son was your teacher in Tibet. He has wonderful teaching skills that he hasn't had the opportunity to use so far." Someday, in this life, he would teach me again. (He was driving trucks at the time.)

He's now teaching me to use the computer to write this book, in spite of my determination to be computer-free. It's taken a lot of patience on his part, but I'm finally getting the hang of it.

And his thriving business—teaching our friends to operate their home computers—has brought us great pleasure from hearing praise about his teaching ability.

The Chauvinist

Audrey, another excellent local psychic, delivered a fascinating "soul-pattern" reading during my first visit many years ago. The reading went back over many lifetimes in a general way. "You have been a man in many lifetimes," she said, "and you were a chauvinist in a lot of them. In this lifetime, you're going to run into a lot of chauvinist males who were the women you treated badly in that lifetime and have come back as males. They're going to treat you the way you treated them."

Yes, indeed.

10
Teaching About Reincarnation

"Marge, am I teaching reincarnation the right way?"
"Honey, your guides are laughing. They're saying, 'Tell her *we're* teaching it the right way!'"
"You mean *I'm* doing all the work and *they're* taking all the credit?"
"What it means, Pam, is that they're helping you to teach people about reincarnation by planting ideas in your mind. But you know you'll always have the free will to teach it any way you want. It's just that their ideas will appeal to you more."

I'd been teaching reincarnation as part of a six-week adult education program. My course was *A Study of Unseen Forces,* an introductory course on astrology, palmistry, psychics, the spirit world, ghosts and reincarnation.

The lecture that made the most profound impression on the class of about forty students was the one on reincarnation. The students couldn't get enough of it. Questions about past lives popped up in all the other classes. So I decided to focus my efforts on a presentation called *The Case for Reincarnation* and offer my services to the masses. Fifty speeches later, I'm so familiar with the material that my hour-long performance needs no notes. Anthony Robbins (a big-name New Age guru) has nothing on me—except higher speaking fees.

One of my speeches made history: the largest United Church in the area invited me to speak about reincarnation. As I informed the audience, this lecture was probably the first lesson on reincarnation taught in a Christian church *in fifteen hundred years*—without exaggeration. (I elaborate in the speech.)

The occasion of my talk to the congregation was the fifth in an eight-week series of lectures by notable specialists in a variety of disciplines. The large church hall was packed with 160 people at the ungodly hour of 9:15 on a blustery February morning—in spite of snowstorm warnings.

I felt very important. And because I was speaking to a religious audience, nervous.

"I want to thank you on behalf of my bridge club," I said, after the introductions. "They're so grateful I finally have another outlet for this material. They've been the ungrateful recipients of this information for years."

Now, picture the following. Lots of arm-waving for emphasis. Back-and-forth pacing as I tried to remember what to say next. And trying to convince the sleepy audience that reincarnation is a fact.

A big job, in this setting.

What follows is my presentation, adapted for this book.

The Case For Reincarnation

Life is Not Fair!

Some people are born with everything... others are born with handicaps. Some people die in their sleep... others die a painful lingering death. Children die, and bad things happen to good people.

Where is the justice in this?

If there's a just and loving god, it doesn't make any sense ... unless there's more than one lifetime. Maybe one life is like the chapter of a book: it doesn't make any sense until you read the whole thing.

Teaching About Reincarnation

And, we ask, "Why are we here?" How can we exist or have any direction in our lives if we can't answer this question? Or, "Where did we come from? and where do we go when we die?"

I'd like to present the most compelling evidence available in favor of reincarnation, and from these facts show three things: why we're here; how understanding reincarnation helps us lead better lives; and that...

Life is ultimately fair.

I was a big skeptic about life after death. I'd stopped going to church at age thirteen. For the next thirty years, I was an agnostic. Then a friend talked me into going to a psychic. I was so thunderstruck by the reading that I immediately started learning more about reincarnation, psychics, ghosts and such.

I'm a believer now. Not only in a Divine Plan, but also in a Divine Planner, whom I call God.

Reincarnation is the most important concept you'll ever learn. I'm here today to show you why. My speech is in three parts:

1. What are the twin laws of reincarnation and karma?

2. What is the most compelling evidence to support the concept?

3. How does reincarnation work in everyday life and what are the benefits of understanding it?

Reincarnation and the Law Of Karma

Reincarnation, simply stated, is the concept that our *preexistent* souls enter into a series of physical bodies. The purpose is to learn about all facets of human life and from them the lessons we need to grow spiritually. None of us learns from pleasure, we only learn from dealing with problems. Nor can we be truly compassionate unless we've walked in the same shoes as someone else who's having difficulty. Evidence shows that we rest between lives until we decide it's time to come back for more growth. When we've evolved enough (reincarnation is the evolution of the soul), we don't have to return anymore. We become one with the Creator, or God.

We have a *divine* origin, and a *divine* destiny.

The law of karma is the cosmic law of cause-and-effect. Whatever we do comes back to us sooner or later. It is not a punishing law. It's impersonal but immutable. It's a natural law of balance to create harmony, exactly like Newton's law that for every action there's an equal opposite reaction. Karma needs reincarnation in order to work, and vice versa. They are twin laws of the universe. By understanding how they work, we can flow with them in life instead of trying to swim upstream.

Free Will

"What about free will?" is usually the first question I'm asked.

Free will is our greatest gift from our Creator. Our decisions, based on free will, determine whether these twin laws will help us or harm us. If we harm someone, we will eventually suffer the same physical or mental pain that we inflicted. If we're kind and serve others, we reap the benefits. But time is fickle... we don't always see instant results. Souls are not wise enough to deal with instant karma. They need time to learn more about life to gain enough wisdom to deal with it. But sooner or later the long arm of karma will even things out. Nobody gets away with anything—ever.

I'd like to talk about the different kinds of karma.

Boomerang karma: This is the "eye for an eye" kind. If we take an eye, an eye will be taken. Many people think it gives us the right to "take an eye for an eye."

Misuse-of-our-body karma: Taking care of our bodies is another obligation. Our bodies are necessary for our soul's journey on earth. I must have been a glutton in a past life because, in this one, my body forces me to be careful about what I eat.

Symbolic karma: If we've turned a deaf ear to someone's plea for help in a past life, we may be born deaf or hard-of-hearing in this one. That does not mean that everyone born deaf has done someone harm; a person may have chosen to be born deaf in order to learn certain lessons. But it's a possibility. There are few genetic *accidents*.

Continuity karma: Child prodigies have worked on their talents somewhere else before their birth. Evidence from hypnotic regressions and Edgar Cayce's readings indicate this arrangement. Remember— *something* never comes from *nothing*.

Parallel karma: Sometimes we're born with the same injury we've inflicted on another person in a past life.

Shared karma: We're born into families of people we've known before in other roles—either within a former family structure or as friends. Now, when your children complain they didn't choose you for a parent, you can set them straight!

Law-of-grace karma: Good behavior, such as extraordinary service to others, goes a long way to shorten a negative karmic lesson.

What Happens When We Die?

We have two bodies—a *physical* body and a duplicate *energy* body.

When we die, our physical body returns to the Earth, while our energy body, containing our mind/soul and spirit, now unencumbered, speeds up its vibration and moves to the next dimension.

The spirit world functions all around us, but our physical eyes can't see it. We can't see X-rays, TV or ultraviolet waves either, but we know that they exist. Some mediums can see the spirit world easily.

Spirits can visit us whenever they wish but we can't visit them at will. Through sensitive mediums we may be lucky enough to hear from loved ones, but there's no guarantee. When we ask a medium to contact someone, a message somehow goes out into the spirit world. If our loved ones can be reached and wish to talk, they will. And they'll always give us a clue so we'll know who it is. For instance, in my second psychic reading, my grandfather said, "Hi, Pammer." He was the only one who called me by that name.

Great Thinkers Who Believed in Reincarnation

Three-quarters of the world believes in reincarnation, as did some of the greatest minds in history.

Pythagorus, the father of mathematics, ran a school of mysteries that taught reincarnation as well as numerology, astrology and divination etc. in 520 BC.

The neo-Platonic schools of Athens taught reincarnation and flourished for 900 years until the Emperor Justinian closed them up along with the University of Athens. These were the last bastions of reincarnation teaching. Justinian denounced reincarnation at the second council of Constantinople in 553, and reincarnation was suppressed by the Christian religion until the Age of Enlightenment (1700s) in Europe.

Jesus was an Essene, a sect that believed in reincarnation according to the Dead Sea Scrolls. "Jesus said, 'Before Abraham was, I am,'" among other reincarnation remarks he made. Look for them also in the Book of John, Chapter Three, where Jesus, speaking of John the Baptist, says, "And if you will receive it, this is Elijah which was for to come. He that hath ears to hear, let him hear."

Napoleon believed he was Charlemagne, and often publicly stated his belief.

Teaching About Reincarnation

Einstein kept a well-thumbed copy of Madam Blavatsky's book *Isis Unveiled* on his desk. A major thrust of her teachings was reincarnation.

Ben Franklin (my hero) was a scientist, philosopher, statesman and writer. When he was 22, he wrote what some experts consider the most famous epitaph in America—his own. (This appears at the end of Chapter 13.)

For further writings of great minds, I recommend the book, *Reincarnation: The Phoenix Fire Mystery*, by Joseph Head and S.L. Cranston.

Bridey Murphy

The Bridey Murphy case was the story that launched nation-wide interest in reincarnation.

One evening, Morey Bernstein, an amateur hypnotist, regressed a friend by the name of Ruth Simmons after a dinner party at his home. As she slipped back in time, she began to describe a life in Cork a hundred years ago as an Irish woman. Bridey Murphy was her name.

The press had a field day in 1956 when Morey Bernstein's book, *The Search for Bridey Murphy,* was published. (It sold over eight million copies.) Anti-reincarnationists, both scientific and religious, claimed it was a hoax. Most people still have the impression that the Bridey Murphy story was a fake.

Palmer Hoyt, editor and publisher of the Denver *Post,* sent William J. Barker, a journalist, to Ireland for three weeks to conduct a really intensive hunt for "Bridey evidence." His findings appeared in a 19,000-word report titled *The Truth about Bridey Murphy.* It appeared as a special twelve-page *Post* supplement March 11, 1956, and later was widely reprinted in U.S. and Canadian dailies. His extensive investigation showed not only that it was *not* a hoax or deliberate deceit, but also that "Bridey's" facts checked out in most cases (as many as Barker was able to follow up in the allotted time). The bottom line was that the debunkers were themselves debunked.

As a result of popular interest in the story of Bridey Murphy, scientific research began. Past-life therapy emerged using hypnosis to reveal past-life incidents that created present-day problems. The patients are often quickly healed.

Hypnosis had been researched before, but now past-life investigations brought startling relief to people with phobias or other problems. Today, hypnotic therapy is big business.

Hypnotic regression has three main purposes: *instant healing* by finding the source of the illness or phobia; *deep insight* into relationship problems in this life; and *spiritual teaching* by teaching us what it's like between lives and how we make decisions before we're born.

Evidence: Conscious and Unconscious

Until recently, no hard evidence could be found that could be called "proof" of reincarnation. We had to rely on an accumulation of evidence from various sources. This was divided into two main categories: conscious, and unconscious.

Conscious

- Spontaneous memories: some adults momentarily flash back in time and glimpse scenes from past lives.

- Children: 3,000 cases are on file at the University of Virginia of children's conscious memories of past lives.

- Déjà vu experiences: some people, while travelling in foreign countries, know an area they've never before had any information about.

Teaching About Reincarnation

Unconscious

- Dreams: recurring dreams that involve the person's death in another life or that suddenly solve some present day phobia.
- Hypnotic regression: some people have recalled past-life traumas through hypnosis and been healed after only one session.
- LSD psychotherapy: patients often have past-life recalls.
- Automatic writing: some people in a light trance can bring information from other lives through handwriting or typing.
- Mediums can give past life readings that sometimes have documents to back them up.
- Mediums can bring messages from the spirit world about reincarnation.

ಜ ಜ

> Scientists have gathered all the evidence I'm presenting, with one exception.
> —Edgar Cayce

Rudolph Steiner, an Austrian scientist and educator, said that, because of the evidence, the world is now as ready to accept the theory of reincarnation as it once was ready to accept the theory that the Earth is round.

In the following pages I'll discuss four of the most compelling types of evidence: conscious memories of young children, hypnotic regression, past-life teachings from Edgar Cayce, and the remarkable Jenny Cockell story.

Conscious Memories of Children

Dr. Ian Stevenson has been scientifically researching reincarnation for 30 years. Now nearly 80, he is Carlson

Professor of Psychiatry and Director of the Division of Personality Studies at the Health Sciences Center, University of Virginia. He has published nine books on his research since 1966, two of which have been translated into French, German, and Japanese. Sometimes called "the Galileo of the 20th century," he has studied mostly children who consciously remembered details of past lives, providing detailed and accurate information about people who died before they (the children) were born—people they say they once were. He chose children because they can't control the subconscious influence of a lifetime of information. There are nearly 3,000 cases on file at the University of Virginia.

Dr. Stevenson feels there's enough solid evidence for any rational person to believe in reincarnation. His first book, *20 Cases Suggestive of Reincarnation* (University of Virginia Press), details children's memories of their immediate past lives. His second book, *Where Reincarnation and Biology Intersect* (Praeger Publishing), is even more impressive, listing cases where the birthmarks of the children match the autopsy reports of wounds that killed the people the children say they were in past lives. Each case has details that are astonishing. The book summarizes 112 cases of birthmark evidence. The text is somewhat dry to those of us who are non-scientifically inclined but, nevertheless, it is a fascinating read.

The *Journal of the American Medical Association* supported Stevenson's research in a 1975 article, saying that reincarnation is the most logical conclusion based on the evidence he's presented.

Naturally, there are many skeptics, and Dr. Stevenson has answered the most common questions:

"Are these cases fraudulent?"

- There are no financial rewards or publicity.

Teaching About Reincarnation

- Adults can't coach small children in unfamiliar roles. Any parent knows how hard it is to train a three-year-old child to say "please" and "thank you" consistently, let alone to remember forty or fifty details of a past life.
- There were many witnesses—researchers, family, and acquaintances.
- The children's' behavior was too complex for fraud.
- The researchers cross-examined the children for hours. After the questions, the researchers took each child to the train station in the town where they said they had lived and let them find the locations they had recalled. Not one of the children had any trouble finding his home and recognizing his previous family. And many of them knew what had changed since they'd last been there.
- When researchers returned unexpectedly a year later, the details of each child's testimony were the same.

"Were the children fantasizing?"

- Any fantasies were woven around facts which could be verified.

"Did the testimonies come from hidden information?"

- The children were too young for this sort of influence, usually between ages two to six—and some less than two years of age.

"Did the stories come from genetic memory?"
- The children provided too many details of their past lives (up to fifty, in some cases).
- The child testifying couldn't be a descendent of "X" (his former life) because "X" lived in a completely different family and village.

"Were the children using clairvoyance or telepathy?"
- The children provided information or skills connected with only *one* stranger.
- The children could remember how things used to be when they were living in their past-life locations. If they were indeed reading minds, then those minds would know about the changes.

One interesting example of birthmark evidence from Dr. Stevenson's book involves a child in Turkey who remembered being a bandit. He'd committed suicide to escape capture by the French police. He'd done this by jamming the muzzle of his long rifle under his jaw and pulling the trigger. The interviewers found an old man who had witnessed the bandit's death.

In this life, the boy had been born with a huge gash mark under his chin. When the parents gave permission to shave the child's head, a second gash mark just to the left of the crown of his skull indicated a trajectory that was exactly correct for the story of the bandit's death. If such a shooting had happened in this lifetime, the victim wouldn't have lived to tell the tale.

Stevenson's second book contains a picture of this child and many other fascinating color photos of birth defects and unusual marks. Some look like actual scars, other deformities include missing fingers, hands or toes.

Dr. Stevenson feels that there is a direct connection between the number of years between lives and the presence or absence of birthmarks. The interviewed children all had returned within a few years of their former lives. He suggests that something non-physical might convey the scars from one body to another; I believe this is the duplicate energy body I discussed earlier.

Not only is it impressive that medical documents of the deceased correspond to the living child's birthmarks—or in some cases a missing limb or other marks—but it's also hard to come up with other more feasible explanations than reincarnation. People's birthmarks or deformities are more understandable when we know there's a reason.

Consider the children's common characteristics:

- They're usually between two and six years old.
- They often begin by discussing other names and places.
- Their past-life memories usually fade when they're seven or eight.
- They often have a phobia for objects or situations similar to those that caused their deaths. They remember their usually violent deaths clearly.
- Skills that haven't been learned in this life sometimes appear in the children. One example is a perfect dive made by a child on his first-ever attempt. The uncle he'd been in his previous life had been an accomplished diver.
- Sometimes, the children speak foreign languages.

To repeat: the evidence I've just given is by far the hardest, most objective, and most compelling evidence we have so far in support of reincarnation. Keeping this in mind, I recommend a recent book by Carol Bowman, *Children's Past Lives*. It stresses that children can be healed if parents understand that past-life memories might be the source of the problem.

Hypnotic Regression

People have tried to "debunk" hypnosis. But consider:
1. The blind-from-birth can see details of past lives clearly, under hypnosis.
2. Some people can recall historical details that were only later verified.
3. Patients' phobias have been quickly cured (sometimes in one session) when they see the source of the problem in a past life.
4. Some patients speak foreign languages fluently that they've never spoken before.

Dr. Helen Wambach was a noted psychologist based in northern California in the '60s and '70s. Her career consisted mainly of conducting group regressions. She produced two popular books based on her data. Her *Life Before Life* (Bantam Books, 1978) describes 750 hypnotic regressions she conducted, during which she asked participants how decisions were made before they entered this physical lifetime:

1. *Did you choose to be born?*

   95% said "yes," they chose to be born on the basis of advice by other entities.

2. *Did you want to be born?*

   Only 30% said they'd wanted to be born. The rest expressed uneasiness—or in some cases fear—about being able to fulfill the program they'd agreed to tackle in this life.

3. *When did you join your body?*

   At the moment of birth, the response was 33%. Some 15%, who didn't want to be born, said they joined after they'd

been born. (Think of the impact this might have on anti-abortionists.)
4. *Why are you being born?*
The consensus was to complete uncompleted tasks and balance out relationships. Some reported that the right circumstances were available to work on their lessons. (The genetically suitable parents, the appropriate emotional situations and environment.)

Is life predetermined? Dr. Wambach maintains, from her information, that we choose as many lessons as we think we can handle in the lifetime ahead. Some souls are ready to take on more than others. And, apparently, we arrange an easy life from time to time, to renew our enthusiasm for physical life.

Dr. Joel Whitten (M.D., Ph.D.), a neurophysiologist in Toronto, conducted a 13-year program of hypnotic regression research on the state of existence *between* lifetimes. With Joe Fisher, a journalist from Toronto, he wrote a book, *Life between Life* (Dolphin Doubleday), based on the study of 13 contemporary case histories of patients taken back to the state between lives.

He originally stumbled onto this stage of existence during a hypnotic regression where he was trying to take a patient back to a former incarnation. Instead of saying *incarnation* (literally, "in the flesh"), he asked her to go back to her previous *life*. The state of existence she spoke from was entirely new to Dr. Whitten. The first began an enlightening journey that brought fascinating facts from the spirit world where we live between lives. Additional, similar evidence from subsequent patients adds to our knowledge of life between life.

Patients learned several things in common, regardless of their religious beliefs. They all:

- Met loved ones or significant persons during the period between lives.
- Met a judgement board (consisting of three to seven beings) who lovingly reviewed their lives with them.
- Understood why things happened in their present lives.
- Confronted past problems.

All suffered (during this period) the same pain they had inflicted on others in their immediate past physical life.

The patients also learned about choosing their next lives. During states of existence between lives, they learned:

- That the knowledge from past-life reviews helped them decide what situations they needed to grow spiritually in the next life.
- To accept imperfect bodies for their soul's growth. (Not only a lesson in patience, but to have to rely on others.)
- That suicides must return to cope with the same level of difficulty they tried to avoid by ending their lives.
- That group reincarnation allows renewed involvement with people who have figured positively or negatively in former lives.

Many recent researchers provide additional information: *The Case for Reincarnation*, Joe Fisher (Grafton Press); *Reincarnation: A New Horizon in Science, Religion, and Society*, Sylvia Cranston and Carey Williams (Theosophical University Press); *Old Souls*, Tom Schroeder (Simon and Schuster).

Teaching About Reincarnation

Past-Life Teachings from Edgar Cayce

Edgar Cayce (1877-1945) was the most famous and most carefully documented psychic of our time. While self-hypnotized, he gave 14,000 readings, all on record at the Association for Research and Enlightenment (ARE) in Virginia Beach, where he lived.

Cayce was born in Kentucky, and learned as a young man to hypnotize himself. One day, while hypnotized, he diagnosed his own throat ailment and later discovered he could diagnose others while in a trance. Eventually he discovered that all he needed to help people was an address and their presence at that address at the time of the reading. His remedies were often strange but amazingly effective. Castor oil packs were a frequent successful remedy for digestive or reproductive ailments. Some of his followers still employ his recommendations today.

The American Medical Association heard about his abilities and witnessed hundreds of readings. The doctors finally admitted that Cayce was 97% accurate in his diagnoses. This was all the more remarkable because Cayce had only a ninth-grade education. Altogether, he gave 10,000 medical readings.

People started asking other kinds of questions based on his medical accuracy. A close friend of Cayce, Arthur Lammers, long interested in reincarnation, asked Cayce to try past-life readings, an idea sparked by a reading previously given for Lammers where Cayce had ended by saying, "This entity was once a monk."

Cayce objected strenuously to Lammers' request because of his own Christian beliefs. (Cayce not only taught Sunday school, but also read the Bible cover-to-cover every year of his life.) Lammers finally persuaded him that reincarnation information might help people, and Cayce relented. As a result, there are 2,500 past-life readings on file at the ARE and available to everyone, and the many books written about Cayce contain the same information. The book *Edgar Cayce on Reincarnation* (ARE Press) is especially fascinating.

Cayce described past-life actions that affected their present life, providing insight into the reasons behind their problems and helping them to cope more effectively. The readings also explained what lessons the person was here to resolve in this life in order to advance spiritually. (That, he believed, is why we're here)

In many cases, he guided people to their own past-life records that helped to verify his information. These often helped people to discover latent talents that they'd developed in past lives, encouraging people to strike off in a new direction with more confidence.

Cayce's most important points about reincarnation:

- *A soul enters a fetus close to the time of birth,* at the time of birth or sometimes up to two weeks after the child is born.

- *Parents are only a channel* that the soul uses to get to Earth.

- *We do not own our children.*

- *All good* that we do in any life *remains permanently* in our soul's record.

- The *Book of Life* (Cayce calls it the *Akashic record*) for every soul is the substance of the universe (through which radio, TV, and light waves move) that exists all around us and *stores information forever.* This is the source of Cayce's past-life information.

- *Free will is stronger than destiny;* good behavior (service to others) advances souls.

- *Whatever bad situations* we find ourselves in, *we have put ourselves in* by our own defiance of the law (karma and the Golden Rule).

Teaching About Reincarnation

- *The cardinal rule in life is the Golden Rule.* This rule is common to all religions.

There are hundreds of examples of the law of karma (cause-and-effect) at work in the series of books based on Cayce's readings. I mention a few to give you the idea:

1. Prejudice: a man had been a soldier of Gaul in a past life. He'd been taken prisoner by Hannibal and forced to row in the galleys of trade ships. He'd been cruelly treated by black overseers, finally beaten to death by one of them. Cayce told the man it had happened three lifetimes ago and, as a result of this treatment, he had a hatred of the colored race deep in his unconscious.

2. Anti-Semitism: a newspaper columnist had had an intense anti-Semitic attitude for many years that, according to Cayce, came from an experience in Palestine. In that lifetime, he'd been one of the Samaritans who had come into frequent, violent conflict with his Jewish neighbors.

3. Fear of commitment: a 38-year-old unmarried woman had had several romances but was never able to commit herself to marriage. She had a deep-seated distrust of men. Cayce explained that, in an earlier life, her husband had deserted her to join the Crusades.

4. Tolerance: a woman with outstanding tolerance of all religious beliefs had gained this quality while a Crusader among the Mohammedans. She realized that idealism, courage, kindness and mercy exist—even among non-Christians. The impression was so strong that it left her with a lasting sense of religious tolerance.

5. Skepticism in religions: an advertising writer noted for his skepticism in religious matters had been a Crusader in a past life. He was so

profoundly disgusted by the differences between religious profession and practice among the people with whom he'd associated that he had a deep-seated distrust of all external declarations of faith.

Psychiatrists agree that major life attitudes of the psyche arise from the unconscious. Our unconscious (according to Cayce) is where our past-life memories are stored too. Once a person sees the source, the problem promptly disappears.

Cayce's readings also relieved many individuals' phobias:

- *Fear of closed places:* a woman who had no childhood experiences that might have given her this fear was told that she had been smothered in a past life when a cave collapsed on her. Once she learned this from Cayce, the problem immediately went away.

- *Morbid fear of darkness:* one man's fear originated from a dungeon experience in France in the time of Louis XVI.

- *Fear of knives:* this came from the person's having been tortured in France.

- *Fear of wild animals:* this woman's fear started from a life as a gladiator in Rome, being forced to fight wild animals in the arena.

- *Fear of water:* persons with this particular fear had been, in most cases, drowned or shipwrecked.

- *Fear of childbirth:* a woman with this problem had been forced to witness all her children taken and burned to death in 1570 in Carolina.

Cayce's character analyses and descriptions of circumstances of total strangers were correct in thousands of cases, and were accurate at distances of hundreds of miles. His predictions of vocational abilities and other traits in both children and adults proved accurate in later years. Peoples' psychological traits were plausibly accounted for by the past-life experiences Cayce revealed to them.

The data was self-consistent over a period of 22 years, agreeing with itself both in basic principle and in minute detail. This covered hundreds of separate readings taken at different times. Obscure historical details, described by Cayce, have been verified by consulting recorded history. The names of obscure former personalities (the person's past-life name) have been found where the reading had said they could be found.

Readings had a helpful transforming influence on the lives of persons receiving them who followed the advice. The readings were true psychologically, vocationally and physically.

The philosophical and psychological system implied in the readings consistently matches all known facts about mental life. The information suggests new explanations for unexplained facets of mental life. It also agrees with ancient doctrine that has been taught in India for centuries.

Jenny Cockell Story

The story that follows is extraordinary.

All her life, Jenny Cockell had known that she had lived before as Mary Sutton, a young Irishwoman who had died over twenty years before Jenny was born. She constantly dreamed or remembered Mary dying, alone and frantic about what would happen to her eight young children.

Born in 1953, and living in England, Jenny had had a constant sense of guilt and responsibility for the children she'd *left behind*. She had felt there were seven or eight of them, the oldest being about thirteen when she'd died a month after giving birth to her last child.

Over the years, more details of her former life came to her. In her file of dreams and waking visions, she noted:

- a description of the cottage where she had lived with her husband and children
- the remains of the stone supports of the gateway to a nearby house
- the Catholic Church
- the Protestant Church in Church Road
- the butcher's shop in Church Road
- the jetty where she regularly waited for a boat to return
- the Friday market on Moore Street
- the Rotunda Hospital, in Dublin, where she'd died

From her earliest memories, around age four, Jenny had drawn a rough map of the village where Mary had lived. She knew it was in Ireland; over the years, the name Malahide, a town north of Dublin, came to her.

In England, where she lived, she finally found a map that was similar to her own. All the roads she had marked on hers, even the distances, were fairly well to scale. And the station was right where she'd marked it on her own map. This was her first confirmation that the dreams and memories were real. An acquaintance brought up reincarnation as a serious possible explanation for her memories.

During hypnotic sessions, later in life, she recalled a trapped hare that was still alive when they found it one morning. Her oldest boy had been about eleven. The whole family had raced out to the field to see the exciting "catch" for dinner.

Jenny was for many years financially unable to make the trip to Ireland, but she eventually located a Malahide street map, in which all the details matched the ones she had written down on her own. She wrote to various records offices in Dublin and put advertisements in the Dublin newspaper asking if anyone knew the family who lived in the first house on the left side of Swords Road. Then, she compiled a short questionnaire with information gleaned from the street map, and sent it to local historical societies, the Rotary Club, women's groups, and the local council. She composed an advertisement for an Irish magazine, asking for help with her research.

Her first opportunity to go to Malahide came in June 1989—she hoped to walk around and find specific details and landmarks. On that first trip, she found most of the landmarks on her list. The visit convinced Jenny that there was enough confirmation to try even harder.

At length, information in response to her advertisement set Jenny on the right track. The name of the family who'd lived in the little cottage she'd described was "Sutton," and a contact she'd made in Ireland could now search for the right records.

Apparently, Mary Sutton's children had been sent to various institutions after her death, and had lost contact with each other. Jenny wrote hundreds of letters of inquiry until she eventually collected copies of the marriage and death certificates, and the baptismal records of six of the children.

Finally, in 1990, after years of effort, Jenny contacted the eldest son, called Sonny, who wondered how she could know so much about him, particularly Jenny's description of the morning they found the trapped hare, Sonny agreed to help her find the other siblings. With Sonny and the daughter of another brother, Jenny was able to track down six of her past-life children who were still alive, in their fifties and sixties. The reunion was televised, and a drama of the story played recently on the British PBS network.

Jenny's need to reunite her past-life children started the long search that resulted in an amazing reunion.

Reincarnation and Karma in Everyday Life

So far, I've described the twin laws of reincarnation and karma, and discussed three kinds evidence. I'd now like to show how reincarnation and karma work in everyday life.

Although we see both positive and negative karma happening all around us every day, negative karma does not always mean that a person is suffering an "eye for an eye" kind of karma. The negative event affecting someone may have been chosen, with guidance from loving entities in the spirit world, for spiritual growth, before he or she was born.

Personal Karma

Before birth, we choose the way we're born and the way we die. The long periods of suffering that some of us may experience before death teach us compassion for others suffering through a similar situation. Remember that our soul uses *free will* to choose our lessons *before* we're born. After we're born, we continue to use *free will* to deal with each lesson.

Elvis Stoyjko, a figure skater, said in an interview after he lost a championship, "We don't always get what we want, but we always get what we need."

We choose our sex and sexuality—male, female, homosexual, asexual—for the experiences the various roles will bring. The older the soul, the more balanced the male-female qualities will be from many lifetimes spent learning nurturing as well as aggressive roles. We all know some couples where the father is far more nurturing than the mother.

Some homosexual males may have had many lifetimes as women, and now have decided it's time to learn masculine skills. In this lifetime they may still be so attached to the female role and to men as sexual partners that they can't make a complete transition. Other homosexuals may be born that way because,

Teaching About Reincarnation

according to Cayce, they had mocked homosexuals in a former life. Whatever we mock, we become, he says.

We all experience life in different races. Under hypnosis, people see themselves in different skin colors. Cayce's readings report similar findings. This refutes the DNA theory of memories of past lives. Scientists who are determined to argue against reincarnation claim that past-life memories are passed down through our genes—but how can that be if we change races?

Suicide may seem like merely a convenient exit, but a soul must come back and face the same situation again. The next time around, a person may have enough memory in his subconscious to know that suicide is *not* the easy way out.

Sometimes, we choose to be born with deformities. Somehow we choose the genetic situation in our parents that will bring this about. There are many possible reasons for such deformities: a lesson in *patience*, learning to rely on other people (or relinquishing control), a memory from a past-life injury, and so on. Or "payback time" for an injury inflicted on another—we've each presumably taken part in a war or two.

All illnesses have a cause, sometimes to teach us patience, or perhaps to slow us down. Sometimes an illness forces us to take a new direction in life.

When parents give birth to a mentally "retarded" child, the lesson is usually for the parents. If the child is loved, it is usually happy. Before birth, it had agreed to play this role. Cayce explains that the brain is like a radio through which our mind/soul (the radio station) functions. If the radio doesn't work, that doesn't mean the radio station is faulty.

If we're born with skin allergies, we may have been "thick-skinned" in a past life, according to Cayce. A victim of a dust allergy was told in a reading that he had left people to die in a desert windstorm.

We plan some specific events before we're born. Sometimes we decide with our spiritual advisors that an accident will teach us a necessary lesson.

One woman saw, under hypnosis, that she had planned a life-altering event, which was to happen when she reached the age of forty. At age forty, in this life, she was raped. The effect of the assault changed her occupation from business to helping other rape victims for the rest of her life.

People marry for happiness. Cayce says the purpose of marriage is to resolve past life conflicts and help each other grow. By understanding that there is work to complete and that happiness is a by-product of this accomplishment, more marriages might last long enough to get through the tough times. Cayce says that the rare, truly happy marriages have been *earned* by hard work on the relationship in past lives. But he also says that some marriages were never meant to *last*. If one partner refuses to work on it, it's sometimes better to separate to avoid more bad karma. However, until the two finally resolve their problems, they'll meet again and again with the same difficulties.

Most of us have experienced meeting someone for the first time and instantly feeling comfortable. This is simply a reunion with someone we've known before.

Sometimes a person who's happily married meets another of the opposite sex and a powerful mutual attraction develops. It's usually someone outside the person's social circle and there's frequently an age gap, a racial difference, or a different religion. These attractions are a carry-over from a previous life, and sometimes bring unfinished business with them. Cayce cautions us about breaking up a marriage over such attractions. But by understanding what's happening, a person can better handle the feelings.

We've all at least heard of "love at first sight." Meeting someone you feel you've known forever is so common that the song *Who Knows Where or When* became very popular years ago. Karma reaches out its long arm for lovers too.

Teaching About Reincarnation

Cayce told several people who came for readings that they couldn't have children in this life because, in past lives, they either failed to nurture the ones they'd had or they'd abandoned or mistreated them. Only our souls know the real reason behind the events in our lives. Sometimes a good psychic can see the reason. Hypnosis, as we discussed earlier, is also effective.

The death of one's child is the biggest "why?" of all. The child is usually an old soul (having wisdom gained from hundreds of lives lived) that has agreed to come to Earth briefly to teach the parents, by appearing to leave too early, a lesson in grief. When we read about a child who has died from a lingering illness, the description of the child is in every case similar: "wise beyond her years," "he seemed to easily accept that he was going to die," "she'd say, 'Don't worry, Mom, I'll be happy in Heaven,'" "he made everyone around him happy," "she was a very special person." Watch for these reports the next time you read of a child who has died, particularly from a long illness.

Cayce explains Sudden Infant Death Syndrome: a soul realizes it has misjudged the situation into which it chose to be born. It withdraws to wait for a more appropriate body for its Earthly lessons. Cayce says this is why, in some cases, no physical cause of death is found.

We must keep learning all our lives. Getting old is simply approaching the end of a chapter in our "book of life." The more we learn in this life, the more we'll know in the next. Elisabeth Kübler-Ross says that 80% of elderly people in America are depressed "because they think death is the end. If they understood the concept of reincarnation they might be more active and make the best of their remaining years in their present body."

Once the initial pain of loss has eased, it's best to let the grief go as soon as possible. Grieving holds back the loved one's growth in the spirit world. But spirits do love to have their photos displayed around a home, to remind us to think about them. Prayers that send them on their way with love are important, too.

Social and Ethical Karma

Capital punishment is a denial of the law of karma. We have no right to take another life except in self-defense, or to defend another person or a country. If someone is dangerous to others, then it's a matter for the courts to decide. But if a murderer gets off because of a technicality, then karma, the divine law of balance, will eventually even the scales. He'll have to suffer the same pain he inflicted, not only on the victim, but also on the family and friends of the victim. "God is not mocked," quotes Cayce from the Bible.

Rabbi Yonassan Gershom wrote a wonderful book, *Out of the Ashes* (ARE Press). He comments on the Holocaust in connection with reincarnation and the law of karma. He says the victims of these crimes "didn't necessarily ask for it." He explains that we choose a general outline in order to leave room for our free will and the free will of others. He feels that some Jews may have chosen to be martyrs in this life to teach the world about evil on a large scale, so that such events may never happen again. Others had the opportunity to escape and refused it. Some may have been warriors who raped and pillaged during battles. The important point is that each soul had its own reasons to return.

If the motive is to help people, genetic meddling isn't bad. In the case of *in vitro* fertilization, a soul will only join the fetus—created outside the womb—if it wants to. If it doesn't, it won't. So where is the harm? Cloning can be reconciled using the same reasoning.

Passive euthanasia is acceptable, in my opinion, if the motive is to relieve suffering. If the soul wants to leave, it will. Cayce explained that often a soul has already left the physical body before the body has stopped functioning. Once the body can't help the soul learn more lessons, it appears, from the evidence, that it's all right to let it go. And in my opinion, if a person is suffering intractable pain, it is cruel not to give them enough medication to make them comfortable—even if it means they may become unconscious or there is a risk of death. Remember the Golden Rule.

According to Cayce, abortion is the destruction of the temple of the soul—not of the soul itself. He says the soul enters the fetus close to the time of birth, and sometimes the soul moves in and out before the final decision to stay. Sometimes it enters a couple of weeks before birth, sometimes at the time of birth, or up to two weeks after birth. This obviously means that an early abortion does not dispatch a soul from its fetus at all. The soul comes from somewhere else to join the fetus—mothers don't walk around with multiple souls in their bodies. If the fetus is destroyed and the soul has already entered, it simply withdraws and returns to wherever it came from. From there, it waits for another more suitable vehicle for its lessons.

The knowledge of reincarnation gives us new insights. A colossal portion of humanity is morally and ethically confused. The churches have had two thousand years to teach us why we're here, where we come from, and where we go when we die—and they've failed miserably. A Catholic priest answered my question, "What is the purpose of life?" with the simplistic answer, "To love God." What does *that* mean?

The two most important benefits of understanding reincarnation are:

- Knowing how important it is to live by the Golden Rule (because whatever we do to someone will be done to us).

- Knowing how important it is to help others and to be kind. The end result is a nobler life lived.

Happiness is not the goal in life, but the by-product of a job well done—a lesson learned, a kindness bestowed, or the deserved love of friends and family. We're in school, here on Earth, to learn and to grow. That's why life is so hard: nobody ever *learns* from pleasure. We only grow through pain in our lives. Too many people think life is play, resulting in a meaningless race for "things" to make us happy. Fran Lebowitz, a New York writer, contends that middle-class Americans take Prozac, and poor Americans illegal drugs, because they're depressed. They have no meaning to their lives. This emptiness leads to mindless violence, addictions, and suicide. The suicide rate among students in America has tripled in the last 20 years. Depression and melancholia are rampant. Too many youths today turn life's "speed bumps" into unscaleable peaks. They have no understanding that we're meant to work through our difficulties or to work around them. They just give up.

There's no hurry in life to accomplish things. We never run out of time! What we don't get done in this life we can do in the next, or in the one after that. This knowledge has helped me to slow down and stop worrying about what I thought I'd never be able to do. Now, I concentrate more carefully on the present and enjoy it more.

Donating organs is like passing along our old clothes to someone who needs them. Now that we've learned that our soul doesn't need our physical body after we die, it's almost immoral *not* to donate our body parts.

If everyone thought this way, think how many more people could be helped.

What If the Whole World Believed in Reincarnation?

There could be a tremendous change in behavior! For instance:

- *Fewer wars:* If everyone understood that group action against an enemy (except in self-

Teaching About Reincarnation

defense) will generate similar action in return, sooner or later, war plans might be modified or eliminated.

- *Fewer crimes:* Nobody gets away from the long arm of karma: whether the criminal gets caught or not, he or she will eventually suffer the same consequences. Knowing that beforehand might be a deterrent.

- *Greater respect for others:* We'll all be in someone else's shoes sooner or later. Rich, poor, sick, a different race, color, sex and so on. Knowing of that possibility might create more tolerance and a gentler world climate.

- *More ethical business and politics:* If businessmen and politicians know that reincarnation is a fact, they might function at a higher ethical level. Miracles can happen!

- *Doctors might reconsider life support systems:* Once doctors understand that when a soul wants to go, it's better to let it go. This will save the health system a lot of money.

- *Suicides might decrease:* Once potential suicides understand that there's no escape because we never die and that he or she will have to come back to face the same situation again, they may reconsider ending it all.

- *Homosexuality might be accepted and understood:* When everyone understands that we will all be born homosexual at some time in our own soul's journey, genuine fellowship toward homosexuals might prevail.

- *Racial slurs* might disappear for the same reason.

- *Religious elitism:* "My way is the only way" will end when spiritual enlightenment comes to the whole planet. Understanding reincarnation and karma is a major start in the right direction.

- *More kindness and generosity in the world*: When we learn that every little act of genuine kindness stays forever in our "Book of Life," we're bound to make a better effort.
- *Self-discipline*: With awareness of long-term (next-life) consequences, people might be more inclined to avoid the bad karma that gluttony, alcoholism, drugs, uncontrolled rage, psychological abuse, and so on will attract. The Golden Rule will be taught in schools, churches, and homes.

Until we change ourselves, wars and other outrageous behavior will never end.

The Purpose of Life: Love, Laws, Lessons

Our souls have three important reasons for being here.

1. We're here to love others unconditionally—not "I'd love you if only...."—and we're here to serve others, because the more we serve, the more we grow spiritually.

2. We're here to learn and grow in understanding of the unseen laws around us, so that we can live in harmony with them. Learning about reincarnation is a great start. Reincarnation and karma explain why the Golden Rule is so important.

3. We're here to deal with the lessons we've chosen to work on in this lifetime.

Ben Franklin

I promised, at the beginning, that I would read Ben Franklin's famous epitaph. He wrote it when he was twenty-two. Although it was never carved on his stone, it is still considered the most famous epitaph in America.

BEN FRANKLIN'S EPITAPH:

The Body of B. Franklin
Printer,
Like the Cover of an Old Book,
Its Contents Torn Out
And
Stripped of its Lettering and Gilding,
Lies Here
Food for Worms,
But the Work shall not be Lost,
For it Will, as He Believed
Appear Once More
In a New and more Elegant Edition
Revised and Corrected By the Author.

Life is Fair

When we accept the law of karma—cause and effect—we understand that life is not a series of random events. And this gives us the gumption and endurance to get through tough times.

But, most important of all, we learn that there are no injustices in life—that life has justice, meaning, and purpose. After all of a person's lives have been lived, we know that the negatives and positives will have been balanced. And we know that, ultimately, *life is fair!*

☙ ☙

Having expended all that hot air during my allotted hour, I was ready for a drink, but it was only 10:15 in the morning. So, instead, I answered the barrage of questions from the fifty raised hands in the audience.

If they had so many questions, you, the reader, probably do, too. At the back of this book, I've added a suggested reading list. It's a cross-section of books that I have enjoyed. Some of them contain true testimonies. Others give more in-depth information about the basics that I've just discussed.

11
Ghosts

The Face in the Photo

"I've got a picture of you and Dave that I took at the cottage last week," said my friend Carole. "There's the weirdest face over your shoulder—it's really creepy. I'll bring it to bridge next week."

We had just spent a weekend with two other couples at Carole's cottage. The day the picture was taken, the six of us had been discussing astrology from Linda Goodman's book *Sun Signs*. Everyone enjoyed hearing his or her own characteristics, and from there the conversation roamed to other occult topics. So, mysticism was "in the air" that day.

Carole had little interest in "mysterious things"—tending to roll her eyes whenever I mentioned any strange topic in my repertoire. So I was doubly curious about the "face."

The photo showed an older, hooded and bearded male face gazing into the camera over my left shoulder. A later, enlarged photo produced an even sharper image of the face. But, adding to the mystery, Dave's and my faces were *fuzzy* while the background and the ghostly figure were clear.

"I feel it's a grandfatherly person from a past life," said Marge, holding the picture, "but I can't get any more than that."

Ghostly photographs have been recorded for years. Many books show partially visible images with testimonials to their authenticity and accompanying stories behind their appearance.

As far as Carole knew, the "face" picture had not been double-exposed or tampered with.

Another Ghostly Image

Mary's husband Paul took my picture, at Mary's request, after my third or fourth reading. The Polaroid shot developed as we stood talking. A blurry oval moon appeared where my face should have been, while my shoulders and the background were sharp and clear. Odd, I thought. Mary held it and said, "A ghost. Don't show it to people. Bad luck." She didn't elaborate, and I didn't know enough at the time to ask more questions.

The Tape

With my speech propped up on a music stand in front of me, I was all set to begin, when a woman sitting on my right said, "Excuse me, you don't mind if I tape the speech, do you?"

Yes, I did. But she'd taken me by surprise.

Thirty women circled the large living room in which I was about to speak. The woman who had just asked the question was a close friend of the hostess. I paused, thinking, *no, I don't want it taped*, but I gave in to avoid any awkwardness.

I'd honed my speech to a performance that eliminated any glazed looks—and I didn't want anyone else using it. But I remember Marge summing up a reading a few months previous, saying, "Pam, it'll go the way it's supposed to go." Trusting her words, I launched into my lecture.

At the end of my talk, the woman with the recorder stood up and said to the room in general, "I can't believe this—my tape recorder is new and so was the tape, but it didn't work."

Marge had told me that sometimes her customers' tapes wouldn't work when they had tried to record her readings. She said, "I'm never sure why, Pam, but there's always a reason."

An Unseen Visitor

Winding up a twenty-fifth sorority reunion lunch, those of us from out of town lingered in our hostess' living room for a few last words. We had started talking about our different interests since we'd last been together, and when I started telling psychic stories everyone got into the act.

"This house has a ghost," said Ann, the hostess. "Every time one of my sons comes into this living room, the fire starts. We always have a few pieces of charred wood left over from a previous fire, but they've been cold for days when it happens. We never have a fire set to light. Besides, everyone with a real fireplace knows how hard it can be to get a fire going in a hurry. When John enters the room, the fire starts right up. Other little things are always happening around the fireplace, too."

As she started to describe them, a loosely crumpled ball of paper that had been sitting in the middle of a large table across the room started rolling toward the fireplace and dropped off the table. "Just like that," she said. We all looked at each other in silence.

No one had been walking in or out of the room to stir the air. The windows were closed against the chilly fall weather. There was no breeze of any kind. And the table was perfectly level. But the crumpled paper had traveled over three feet to get to the edge of the huge table.

A poltergeist (a mischievous spirit described later in this section) probably caused the fires, its energy triggered by the emotional intensity of John. Our focused discussion of ghosts—ten minds thinking the same thought—may have roused the energy of the poltergeist and created the paper ball incident. Or maybe the poltergeist had just wanted to show there really is an unseen world. Who knows? As Albert Einstein said, "He who cannot pause to wonder is as good as dead."

❦ ❦

Evidence of ghosts is solidly based—repeated photos taken of the same ghost, sound recordings with pertinent messages, successful exorcisms captured on videotape, and testimonies by reliable people.

In Europe, a person can break a lease if a house is haunted—this has been understood for centuries. People often conceal a haunting if they intend to sell their house… or, they may just be embarrassed to mention it. Exorcisms by clergy and mediums is a big business in Europe.

❦ ❦

Lori and her husband Joe were sitting in bed the night of his grandmother's funeral, with Benjy, their poodle, asleep in a far corner of the bedroom. Joe was saying how badly he felt that he hadn't been able to say "goodbye" to her. "Suddenly, Benjy stood up shaking and slobbering," said Lori. "He had strings of saliva just pouring out of his mouth. He was looking at something that moved from the door of our bedroom over to Joe's side of the bed. All this time he was whimpering and shaking.

"Then, after a few seconds, his head started to move slowly like he was watching something move back to the door.

"'That's just Grandma, saying goodbye,' said Joe."

❦ ❦

Ghosts are human souls who haven't made the "normal" transition into the spirit world (an experience described by people who've had near-death experiences and have returned to tell the tale). They remain close to whatever it is they can't let go—a person, place, guilt, money, and so on. They are "stuck" here with the living, without their own physical bodies; becoming frustrated, they often turn disruptive. They can be solid and lifelike, partially visible or invisible. Ghosts, whether visible or invisible, can glide through walls and doors. If visible, they usually disappear if followed or touched, and may be observed to gradually grow more indistinct in outline until they finally vanish.

Hauntings extend over a long period of time, with the most common manifestations being sounds: knocks, footsteps, etc. Sometimes spirits move objects, or touch people, or turn lights on and off. (Renovations often stir up a haunting.) These ghosts are sometimes seen or heard by numerous people.

Apparitions differ from haunting ghosts by appearing only once; some last only a few seconds before vanishing. Most apparitions are completely lifelike figures, which can appear solid or translucent. They occasionally glide above the ground and through doors and windows.

Sometimes, the emotional energy of a young person (ten to twenty years of age) will generate rapping, banging, and objects that move when he or she enters a room. This activity is usually called a *poltergeist* (German for "noisy ghost"). When the person leaves the building, the phenomena will follow him to the next location. In all cases, tension—usually anger—is pent up in the young person. These hauntings are usually brief—days, weeks, or months. My friend Anne's son (the story at the beginning of the chapter) started fires when he entered the living room of their home. The phenomenon was absent when her other son came into the same room.

Exorcism may be needed to eliminate the *fear* the ghost creates when it indicates extreme unhappiness or anger (banging doors, wailing, etc.). One method of exorcism (described in Chapter 5) takes advantage of knowing that haunting ghosts are readily attracted to entranced mediums: the medium's altered consciousness allows the ghost to enter the medium's body and speak through him or her. While this is happening, the voice and face of the medium may change to a likeness of the communicating spirit. The medium's partner (who knows what to say to the spirit but is not in trance) must persuade the ghost that it *is* dead.

Ghosts haunt for a variety of reasons.

- *To announce their death*—usually a rather brief "haunting." A mirror cracks, say, or a clock stops, or the apparition appears.

- *Two people have agreed to make contact after one of them has died*—Quite a few have fulfilled this pact, according to the British Society for Psychical Research.

- *Promises not kept by the living can create a haunting*—Unpaid debts or not having a proper burial can make a soul miserable.

- *Souls caught in a "time warp"*—The soul is "fixed" at that point in time, and relives the trauma of its death over and over.

- *The person doesn't realize he or she is dead*—A medium may have to help him follow the "light" (or loved ones) to the spirit world (the state we live in between lives).

- *Sometimes a soul is deranged by the trauma of death*—The ghost cannot perceive the world that awaits him beyond death.

- *Uncompleted tasks from before death*—The ghost may have hidden something before his death, or have left a later "correct" will that he wants found. He or she may have felt upset or guilty about something and wants it resolved. A soul may want revenge for a wrong done to him or a loved one.

Ghosts

"Horses won't go down the Roman line at night" is a common bit of folklore in our area. The road in question had been the scene of the famous Donnelly Massacre in Lucan, Ontario, in the 1800s. People come from all over North America to visit the notorious homestead on the Roman Line.

Sometimes, a whole area seems to be haunted by strong impressions that humans and animals alike can sense. Some experts say the emotional impressions from a conflict may remain in the ether, and become stronger at night when there is less interference from light waves. Sometimes the memories remain in the walls of a building, where different witnesses report seeing or hearing the identical series of events as if they're happening in the present. These impressions seem connected with the combined emotions of the victims and witnesses of the events that took place.

As an example of emotionally saturated walls, Marge told me, "One day some friends I was staying with in Texas took me to see the Alamo. As soon as I stepped in the door, all I heard was the children screaming. I put my hands over my ears and got out of there as fast as I could." Marge was hearing the screams of women and children in the Alamo being massacred 165 years ago by the Mexican army. Marge *never* reads, and knew nothing about the history of the Alamo.

❧ ☙

Many thousands of people who have had a limb or other body part amputated continue to feel the part they have lost—called "phantom pain" or the "ghost limb phenomenon"—even though reason tells them it is no longer there.

A friend of ours, a doctor, described the phantom pain from his amputated limb. "It was worse than any pain I've ever experienced," he said. "I went to Boston for hypnosis and acupuncture treatments, to try and ease the agony, but nothing worked." He went on to say that the medical community claims it's just the severed nerves, still trying to send messages from the amputated limb to the brain. "I think there's more to it than that—but I don't know what. Stories circulate in medical circles of digging up amputated limbs and straightening them out to a normal position to alleviate the phantom pain. I've heard it actually works sometimes."

Earlier, I described our duplicate energy body, which cannot be destroyed. I believe the phantom pain comes from the energy limb still remaining attached to the body where it would normally be. That could explain why an animal will avoid sitting in or walking through the area that, say, a leg would have occupied before the amputation.

Prayers affect ghosts, as do sentiments expressed for them—silent prayers are as effective as those spoken aloud, which shows that human minds continue after death. This could also explain why ghost-hunters have little luck finding their prey, and why spirits seem to leave when ghost-hunters arrive: ghosts may know when to get away. With this in mind, no ghost should be the butt of a joke… or pestered with cameras and tape recorders.

Or, as Cole, the psychic boy in the movie *The Sixth Sense*, says: "They just want us to help them."

12
Stories from Friends and Acquaintances

Eleanor

"I used to wander around in an old cemetery on Main Street on my way home from school," said my friend Eleanor. "I loved to read the names and ages of the children on the tombstones. One day, when I was about eight years old, a bunch of kids I didn't know ran into the cemetery. They didn't go to the only school we had in town. But we exchanged names and ages as kids do, and had a great time playing together. After they'd said goodbye and left, I suddenly realized I'd been talking to the spirits of the children whose names and ages were on the tombstones all around me. They had looked solid and talked as normally as children do. But the names and ages were identical to the markers.

"I was afraid to tell my mother what had happened because she'd think I was crazy."

Eleanor has given me many readings. The children she saw that day may have been attracted by her psychic sensitivity, which allows them to communicate with the living. Whether or not a non-psychic friend might have seen the spirits is not important—the visit from the children, as told by an ethical psychic, reassures us about life after death.

Another Story

"What other psychic pictures did you experience when you were young, Eleanor?"

"During World War Two, when I was about fifteen, I had constant nightmares of people dying. Not soldiers, but ordinary people and children. I could hear the sobbing, and later [after the war] I found out that I was seeing concentration camps. But nobody knew about them until later. When the people died, I saw a curtain lift and angels come to take them home. They went to a beautiful place. It was very reassuring and gave me a peaceful feeling."

Jan

"We had a ghost in our house when we were growing up," said my friend Jan. "But we just ignored him. The house had once been a manse, so we called him 'The Rev.' The noises he made sounded like a man's footsteps walking back and forth along the upstairs hall at night. I didn't hear him as much as my brother and sister did."

"Weren't you frightened?" I asked.

"No, he was just part of the house."

This category of spirit visit is different from Eleanor's. Because it was repetitive, it is referred to as a haunting. A skilled medium could help it move to the normal post-mortal state. Not only would the noises stop, but the soul would be more productive in the next dimension, and at peace.

Aunt Marion

"I remember a couple of odd things that happened," said my Aunt Marion (age 93, with *all* her marbles), in answer to my question about family ghost stories. "I've never talked about it much because they always called you 'fey' in those days if you told weird stories.

Stories from Friends and Acquaintances

"My good friend Vi had just died. For years, she had dropped by in the afternoon or evening for a glass of sherry or wine. The wineglasses we used were on the top shelf of the left kitchen cupboard. One day, about two weeks after she'd died, Al [Marion's husband] and I were having a cup of tea in the kitchen when all of a sudden the cupboard door where the wineglasses were kept started to rattle. The door fit snugly and none of the other doors moved. I asked Al what he thought was going on, and he assured me it was probably a distant train or something like that. And we just let it go.

"One evening a week later, I was sewing or doing ceramics or something by myself in the kitchen, when the same cupboard door started rattling again. So I looked at the cupboard and said, 'Come in, Vi.' And right away the rattling stopped. I think she just came to say goodbye. We never heard another sound after that."

The rattling cupboard is a common type of phenomenon usually caused by a mischievous spirit. But, in this case, the rattling of a significant cupboard, and the stopping of the rattling at the mention of her name, suggests that Vi's spirit came by to say "Hi, I'm okay, and goodbye."

"I've got another quick one to tell, if you've got time," said Aunt Marion. We'd just spent two hours talking about the family's foibles and having a lot of laughs.

"One night, about thirty-five years ago, I was sound asleep on my side, when something poking me in the back woke me up. I rolled over and saw a sort of shadowy figure beside my bed. I couldn't make out who it was. My mother and an old flame of mine had both just died. So I guessed, at the time, that it was one or the other. Anyway, it only happened that one time."

It's unusual for an apparition to touch someone but, because Marion was sound asleep, the visiting spirit must have felt it was the only way to get her attention.

It didn't frighten Marion because, as she admitted, she'd always sensed there was life after death.

Alan

"I had a weird thing happen," said my friend Alan. "When I was twenty-three, I tried to commit suicide and failed—and ended up in the hospital. About thirty days later, after I got home, I was so depressed that I was thinking of trying again. Then I heard a low, audible male voice say, 'Don't do it.' I was frightened, and since that day, I haven't thought of trying it again."

Many cases of vocal warnings, with or without an apparition, have been recorded. Alan's advice probably came from a deceased friend or relative.

Mike

"Dad paid me a visit after he died," said my cousin Mike. "Didn't I ever tell you the story?

"One night, I was out in my workshop trying to decide whether or not to build a boat to enter in a huge boat show that was coming up. I was just sitting there looking at my plans when I felt someone else was there. I looked up and Dad was standing there—right up close. He said, 'No question, of course you're going to win.' I felt tears running down my face. Then he disappeared. So I built the boat with confidence. And I won the competition."

Spirit encouragement and prophecy by a loved one does happen. Fortunately, Mike listened and benefited from his dad's prophecy.

Rob

"In spite of the four murders on this property, I've only seen two ghosts," said Rob, the owner of the famous Donnelly homestead where the grisly massacre took place in the 1800s.

Rob is a deep-trance psychic. I first met him when he gave me a reading while he was self-hypnotized. I'd expected that, with his level of psychic sensitivity, he might have had numerous encounters with haunting ghosts on his property.

"I did have a visit from Johanna, one night," he said. Johanna was the wife of the head of the Donnelly family. "She appeared at the foot of our bed and indicated that I was to go to the basement. It took me a while to figure out what she wanted, but finally I 'twigged' and went to have a look. It was a good thing I did, because there was about to be a serious problem with the furnace. Thanks to her, I caught it in time.

"The other ghost is a man who looks out the door of the barn occasionally while I'm guiding my tour groups around the property. Lots of people tell me they've seen him. And one of my horses must have sensed him too—he doesn't like to go in that barn one bit."

Rob's first ghost was a one-time apparition with a warning, another variety of ghostly encounter. But the old man in the barn is a repeating haunting ghost—a lost soul that needs help to meet his loved ones. The horse's reluctance to go in the barn demonstrates the sensitivity of animals to strange activities in the ether that surrounds us where, according to research, memories of previous emotional events remain forever.

Don

"Oh, yes, there's still a ghost at the Grand Theatre," said Don, an actor and acquaintance. The theatre has a resident ghost by the name of Ambrose Small, who, according to reports in our local newspaper and other publications, occasionally appears around the dressing rooms and lower levels of the theatre.

"One day, while we were rehearsing on stage," said Don, "something strange happened. The seats in the audience, as you know, spring up when no one is using them and the underside is black. When we started rehearsing, I saw no one in the orchestra seats. But as the rehearsal went on, one of the seats went down. It stayed down for about half an hour or so, and then it went up again. I guess old Ambrose had paid us a visit."

Ambrose also needs guidance from a medium to free him from his endless round of haunting at the Grand Theatre. His body was never found, which could be one reason he's stuck in an Earth-bound pattern.

Margie

"Didn't I ever tell you about my friend Doris and the grandfather clock?" said my friend Margie. "About a year after Doris died, her son-in-law, Doug, was about to move her grandfather clock that she had left to me. I'd always felt close to her and missed her a lot, and she'd always liked Doug the best of all her children's partners.

"Doug was about to paint our living room and I'd wanted the clock moved to the opposite corner anyway. It was around three o'clock, the anniversary of her funeral—and about the same time she'd been lowered into the ground.

"The clock hadn't worked for ten years. But just before Doug touched it, it went ding, ding, ding, ding, for ten minutes, and then stopped.

"I guess Doris just wanted to say 'hi.'"

Doris paid only one visit. She is not a haunting ghost, but a soul that has followed the light to the spirit world. She returned for a visit on the anniversary of her funeral to say a final goodbye to the two people she'd felt so close to. Spirits who have moved into the normal state of existence after death are able to visit their loved ones whenever they choose. Unfortunately, it doesn't work in reverse.

Karrie

"My daughter died at eighteen months, after open heart surgery," said Karrie, my dermatologist's assistant. "Her name was Sarah. It was so hard—I went to a bereavement group to try to get over it.

"One evening, after the meeting was over, a woman my age told me about a wonderful psychic who might be able to bring a message from Sarah. I'd never been to a psychic, but I screwed up my nerve and went.

"The first thing the psychic told me was that Sarah said 'thank you' for her half of my gold locket. I burst into tears because nobody had seen me tuck it inside her little party dress when she was in her coffin. I hid it way up inside just before she was buried, so no one would find it.

"No one in the family had known I was going to a psychic. After Sarah had thanked me, she also sent unbelievably accurate messages to my three sisters, and passed on some advice as well. My sisters were so shocked by what they heard they took Sarah's advice."

The greatest gift to a bereaved parent is a message from the child indicating that he or she is alive and well in another place. I hope that someday bereavement groups will guide parents to excellent psychics who are able to convey a message from a deceased child.

Aline

"Which 'voodoo' story do you want?" said my friend Aline, when I called to get details about a story she'd told me years ago—long before I had any spooky stories of my own.

Aline had grown up in Alexandria, Egypt—well-educated in a financially comfortable family. Our husbands had been friends in university and Aline and I met after we both were married. Her stories from growing up in Egypt were entrancing, one of them being the following:

"My girlfriend was the victim of an arranged marriage," said Aline. "She didn't want to marry the man her parents had selected. But, all of a sudden, she found herself violently attracted to him—although she still disliked him. The emotional confusion caused her to constantly argue with her parents.

"Her parents, knowing her behavior was completely out of character, and being aware of some psychic matters, suspected someone might have placed a spell on her. They took her to a medium that handled such cases.

"The medium could see, psychically, that my friend's fiancée had indeed put a hex on her. She led my friend and her parents to a graveyard where they found a package of bones and pieces of paper with writing on them, buried in the earth beside a gravestone of a person unknown to the family. My friend's name, the name of her fiancé, and the name of his medium were written on the three pieces of paper. This and other writing was evidence of an evil voodoo spell.

"The medium proceeded to get rid of the spell as only she knew how, and, from then on, my friend was fine. Needless to say, her parents broke off the engagement."

Voodoo operates on the same principles as prayer. It is focused thought directed at an individual. The more people who focus their thoughts on one objective or person, the more powerful the energy. Prayer is directing positive thoughts while voodoo is often used for nefarious purposes. Mediums who know voodoo have special words and objects as well as knowledge of certain procedures to heighten the energy directed at the recipient. Once a spell has been cast on a person, only someone with knowledge of such things can get rid of it.

Stories from Friends and Acquaintances

Lydia

"My mother had a dream that came true," said my friend Lydia. "She was a volunteer nurse for the Red Cross in France in the First World War. In her dream, she was standing on a cliff looking out at the water where her brother-in-law, a doctor, with his three children, were struggling to get to shore in a rowboat. The water was rough. He was making no headway because he'd lost an oar. The oldest son went over the side trying to reach it and drowned. The doctor felt helpless because he couldn't save him. And my mother felt helpless in the dream.

"The next day, my mother got a cable from her brother-in-law saying that all three of his children had polio and the oldest one had died."

Precognitive dreams are prevalent. Before the *Titanic* left the docks on its fatal voyage, over three hundred people called the shipping lines to report that they'd dreamed the ship would sink.

Gina

"One of my twin boys, I'm positive, is my late father," said Gina, my periodontal hygienist. We'd discussed, over previous visits, many psychic subjects. "I don't even mention this feeling to my husband, even though he's Indian, because he'd think I was daft. But I was curious about what you'd think."

"It's quite possible. But what makes you think so?"

"He has the same birthmark on his back that my father had. His personality is the same as my father's and totally different from his twin brother's. My father was an avid boxer, but I'd never discussed the fact with my son. But suddenly my son is crazy about it, too. He even used some of the same gestures and expressions as my dad, although he'd never met him—my father died two years before he was born."

Gina is not crazy. I encouraged her to read Dr. Ian Stevenson's book, *Where Reincarnation and Biology Intersect*, that discusses 110 cases of birthmark evidence—just to reassure herself about her feeling.

Sandy

"Wait 'til you hear *my* story," said my friend Sandy, as she wheeled our golf cart up to our next shots. "One day, when David [her son] was around four years old, he was playing on the kitchen floor while I started to get dinner. He'd been 'good as gold' all day. Suddenly, at five o'clock, he stood up and ran into the living room screaming, 'Daddy, Daddy, I want my daddy!' I couldn't figure out what was going on. I comforted him as best I could, but he fretted constantly over the next hour or so. Then the phone rang. It was Jack [her husband], who told me he and his friend had had a car accident on their way home from the ski hills near Georgian Bay. The accident had happened at about five o'clock."

Many of us have had telepathic situations in our lives. But when a child senses something as strongly as David did that day, it shows that even a young child with no previous knowledge, of such things as bad roads or a snowstorm, can sense an emotional event not only the same time it's happening, but also many miles away.

Tom

"It was just a routine flight from Edmonton to Toronto," said my cousin Tom, a captain for the largest Canadian airline. "It was a boring flight for about two hours. Then, all of a sudden, around four o'clock, I felt something was wrong. First I checked everything in the cockpit—didn't find a thing. Then I got up and searched the rest of the plane, front to back. Nothing. Went back up to the cockpit and landed the plane without any problems.

"After we'd landed in Toronto and checked in, I made a phone call. The person I'd called told me that one of my best friends had died at four o'clock."

Cousin Rob

"I saw a space ship in 1955, when I was twelve years old," said my cousin Rob. "After school—about 4:30—a friend and I were walking west on our way home. The sun was out. We were pushing and shoving each other around as boys do, when suddenly, ahead of us, at about a 45-degree angle, we saw a saucer-shaped flying object with a round dome on top. It was about the same distance away as an ordinary commercial plane, so it was easy to see. It slowly zigzagged for about five minutes and then suddenly took off—a hundred times faster than a plane—and disappeared

"My buddy and I ran home to tell our moms. Mine wasn't home, so we ran next door and told a neighbor.

"The next day, our local newspaper ran an article on page two indicating that many other people had reported seeing it, too."

Flying saucers have been reported as far back as the Old Testament—Ezekiel saw wheels "in the middle of the air." As a stranger standing ahead of me in a line once said, "I used to laugh at any mention of flying saucers, until the day I saw one, up close, near my home. Now I'm a believer."

A Stranger at a Party

"As a former nurse, have you ever experienced an unusual deathbed vigil?" I asked a new acquaintance I'd just met toward the end of a large party. The opportunity followed a discussion of my upcoming book.

"I didn't have any with my patients," she said, "but I did with my own father when he was dying. He'd been slipping in and out of consciousness for quite a while toward the end. But suddenly, he opened his eyes, turned to me and said, 'What am I doing back *here*? I liked it better where I was.'

"He died soon after," she said.

Non-believers in an afterlife may suggest that the gentleman was hallucinating. However, his statement is similar to the testimonies of somewhere between eight and thirteen million people who have been clinically dead and resuscitated.

The Neighborhood Butcher Shop

Within a week after hearing the previous story, I bumped into an acquaintance whose writing course I'd taken several years ago and who later had helped me write a brochure for my lectures.

The cozy shop—where half my social life takes place—was cramped for *any* discussion let alone the one we were about to have. People were "excuse me-ing" around both of us as we talked.

After breaking the news about my book and briefly explaining the content, she offered me the following story.

"My mother had the most amazing passing," she said. "First, I have to explain that she wasn't a religious Jew. She told her grandson, in response to his question about life after death, that she had 'no idea' whether there was life after death, but one day she'd know the answer.

"As she lay dying, her final day, four of us stood by in her bedroom—my sister and I, a nurse, and a homemaker. She'd been lying with her eyes closed for hours. Suddenly, she woke up and stared right into my sister's eyes as she stood at the foot of the bed. Then she shifted her intense stare to the corner of the room where she seemed to be looking at someone or something of great importance to her. At that moment, her breathing changed, from labored to slow and steady. She seemed calm. A peaceful look came over her, and soon after she was gone.

"But an equally interesting thing happened after her body was removed from the house. In the Jewish religion, a volunteer group of people, mainly medical professionals, called the *Chevra Kadisha*, washes the body and sits with it all night before the next-day funeral. They are anonymous and discreet. But one of the women, who'd known mom and had been there when they'd brought her body in, spoke to me at the funeral. She said she gasped at the peaceful expression that was on my mother's face. Jews are not embalmed, as you know, so Mom's expression had no artificial source. In all the years she'd been serving on the committee, she'd never experienced a similar look.

"After being with Mom while she died, I'm now convinced there must be something more after death than I'd thought."

Deathbed scenes reported from all over the world often transcend the religious beliefs or non-beliefs of both the participants and the witnesses.

༄ ༅

These stories demonstrate how close to home, and frequently, mysterious phenomena happen. Once I openly discussed my interest in unseen forces and mysterious things, people talked to me (usually privately) about spooky events in their own lives. I've had some fascinating discussions as a result. You could, too.

Reactions to My Interest in Reincarnation and Psychics

Nothing livens up a dinner party conversation faster than the revelation of a personal psychic prediction—particularly one that's come true—or the lighthearted mention of a past life.

Reactions by people over the last twenty years to my open interest in "the mysteries" have provided regular daily entertainment. They vary from the "scientific" snort of derision, to, "can I call you at home to get the name of the book or psychic?"

My irreverent friends, who've never read a book on reincarnation, allow me one minute at a time to discuss my newest discovery in the field. However, along with my husband, they've sharpened my arguments and my sense of humor. Their indifference, however, has forced me to discuss it elsewhere—with amusing results.

The Cleaning Woman

Lydia was six weeks into her duties. She was gentle, kind, and ladylike (my mother's ideal). Things went smoothly until, one morning, she entered the kitchen and overheard me discussing a psychic with a friend. I glanced up at her—ashen face, rigid body—staring at me as if I'd smacked her with a wet fish.

"What's wrong, Lydia?" I asked after hanging up.

"Was that a fortune-teller you were talking about?" she timidly asked.

"Yes, it was."

"My church says they're the work of the Devil."

"What is your religion?

"Pentecostal."

"If hearing about them bothers you, I won't discuss them again while you're in the house."

Two weeks later, she left a note behind saying she wouldn't be back. She was "allergic to our dog."

Six months later, we met coming from opposite directions on a wide sidewalk.

"Hi, Lydia."

"Hi, Mrs. Evans."

She turned her head away, stepped onto the grass and circled me in a ten-foot radius to avoid my devil's emissions. I loved it.

A New Cleaning Woman

Lydia's departure started a search for a substitute. A pleasant stranger, recommended by a friend, came soon after. The first day on the job, she spent a long time upstairs without making the usual cleaning noises. When she came down, she asked me about the books that filled a wall up there.

"They're books about psychics and reincarnation," I said.

"Oh."

Next week, she examined the books on assorted religions on the main floor. This time, she seemed really disturbed.

"Aren't those books dangerous?" she asked, looking very worried.

"Oh heavens, no," I said. "Those books help you get a better overall picture of all religions, so you can make up your own mind."

"I talked to my pastor after I was here last week, and he told me not to look at them."

By this time, I suspected she would be leaving, so I said, "The more spiritual information you read, the more certain you may be about your own religion—by the way, what is it?"

"Jehovah's Witness."

"Do you go door-to-door?"

"Yes."

The next day, she called and said, "I can't come back, Mrs. Evans, because I'm afraid your books might attack me."

A Scientific Acquaintance

"Whatever you do," said a friend at a party, "don't discuss reincarnation with Helen [not her real name]," who was standing on the other side of the room.

"Why?" said I, perking right up.

"She's a famous scientist, you know, and doesn't believe in any of that psychic stuff."

"Really," said I, already with a half-formed question in my head.

"Helen," I said, "who would I contact at the University to inquire about teaching reincarnation?"

First a noise resembling a snort issued forth, with a look that said, "Did I hear what I thought I heard?" Then the first question: "What degrees do you have?"

I have about five fewer degrees than she does, and it was quickly established I wouldn't qualify for anything on campus, in her opinion.

Not always having the wisdom to walk away graciously, I dug in my heels to start a discussion on reincarnation. Finally, I had to defend myself by saying, "Helen, I'm not a fool, I wouldn't stand here and discuss a subject that I couldn't support with solid research. I've probably researched my field as long as you have yours. I wouldn't presume to tell you your research is faulty because I have respect for what you've done. Have you ever studied *any* research on the topic?"

"Well... not exactly."

"That's not a very scientific approach."

About two years after that discussion, both our names appeared on the same pamphlet, advertising speakers for an eight-week series of lectures to a large audience in town. I *do* hope she read the flyer.

I feel that the fast lane to ignorance is contempt prior to investigation.

An Irate Editor

In response to a second reading of a few chapters of this book, I received an unforgettable report from a Canadian publishing company.

The editor accused me of religion-bashing, poor spelling, punctuation, syntax, attitude—you name it. And my colossal presumption that reincarnation was the reason for everything was the final straw: she said I should "make people look up the meaning of the word 'occult' instead of defining it 'on the fly.'" (I'd used the word "hidden" in brackets). She advised me to get an editor and get my act together before sending my manuscript out again.

I'd heard that sort of rant before, usually after speaking in public. The original editor, who'd loved the first chapter, put a note of apology on the bottom saying that this woman had had a hard life, but in spite of it, kept on smiling.

I steamed for a day and a night before replying. In my e-mail, I apologized for upsetting her and mentioned that my editor found her remarks puzzling.

The Librarian

For years, I'd tried to generate a glimmer of interest in reincarnation in our local librarian's eye. There's something about academics that brings out the devil in me. We're both certain we're right, for starters. But with her rapid-fire speech and skeptical tone, she'd brushed off any discussion as trivial and hardly worth her academic consideration. "I'd have to have a lot more evidence than that," she'd say. Besides, she was always busy on the job. Nevertheless it was a weekly challenge, if I had nothing better to do.

Now that she's retired, I don't see her anymore—until recently, when we met on the street. She made the mistake of asking what I was up to. Slogging twelve blocks together through sugary snow on icy sidewalks, she began asking questions not only about my book, but also about reincarnation. Huffing along—sometimes in Indian-fashion on the narrow path—against the freezing wind, blotting my dripping nose constantly and shouting over the traffic noise, I filled her in on Dr. Stevenson's evidence. At her destination, she stopped and said, "I guess I'll have to get that Stevenson book out of the library."

A major victory—in my own eyes.

Radio Show

It's one thing to bore one's family, friends, and the classes I taught, but another to go on the radio for the first time with a topic like reincarnation, psychics, and such.

My interviewer was entertaining, but had no knowledge of the subjects at hand. He'd asked me to make a list of questions, which he disregarded once we were on the air. The manager was listening carefully; he'd warned me. I donned my earphones with sweaty hands.

A flood of interested calls came in, covering a variety of topics. I was prepared with my notes fanned out in front of me in my tiny, separate booth. Many of the callers inquired about reincarnation. Only one "work of the Devil" call came in during the hour we were on. The manager was happy. I was asked to do six more shows.

Walking back to my office, I alternated between feeling euphoric at the positive reception and weepy that I'd been taken seriously.

TV Show

A few years ago, a local community television show invited me be the sole guest, for two hours, to talk about reincarnation. The interviewer was a friend and a skeptic, but he was desperate.

Much to his surprise, thirty-seven phone calls came in—more than they'd ever had before. But one in particular remains in my mind. A caller described an out-of-body experience he'd had during an anaesthetic, in exquisite detail. When he'd finished, he admitted he'd never told anyone about it because he wasn't sure whether he'd imagined it or not. But when he'd heard the other callers talk about their experiences, he felt he wouldn't be laughed at. We told him we were grateful he'd called.

Stories from Friends and Acquaintances

Two Strangers on a Train

Stepping down from a train at a suburban station near Toronto, I was accosted by two middle-aged women dressed in "librarian" styled beige and gray outfits, accessorized with drab hair, rimless glasses, large tote bags, and unfortunate shoes.

"Excuse me," said the first one, taking a baby-step toward me, "we noticed you were reading a book on ghosts."

"Yes, I was," I said, pulling it out of my bag.

"We just wanted to warn you that if you ever encounter a ghost, you must never, never touch it."

"I've read that somewhere," I said, "something to do with energy flow."

Handing me a pamphlet, she said, "We're always here for you if you run into trouble; we meet on Wednesdays."

When I turned away for a moment to speak to someone behind me, they vanished. Returning to whatever ring of Saturn they'd come from.

A Minister in a Small Town

During a reception after a family funeral, I had a chance to ask the minister, a woman, if her parishioners ever asked about reincarnation.

"Some of them have brought it up," she said.

"What do you tell them?"

"Not much, just that it's not in our teachings," and she turned to talk to someone else.

Over five hundred books exist on the subject—sooner or later, the church is going to have to address the issue.

The Minister from New York

A superstar minister was in town to conduct a friend's mother's funeral. He'd been a well-loved orator at a large church in London before New York lured him away. His dramatic presentations were loaded with quotes from every famous writer under the sun. Spellbound men and women packed the church every week to hear his Irish lilt. I'd heard about him for years, but we'd never met. Now was his chance.

Elbowing my way through the crowd of admirers telling him how wonderful he was, I introduced myself.

"I wonder if I could ask you a question," I asked, looking as innocent as I could.

"Certainly," he smiled.

At the mention of the word "reincarnation," he swiveled away to speak to *anyone* else at hand, faster than Gary Cooper in the movie *High Noon*.

A Minister in a Big City

A stranger to the family conducted my mother-in-law's funeral. At the packed reception, back at her house, the wake had been well underway for the past hour-and-a-half when my husband said to me, "We can't really relax and take off our jackets while the minister's still here. But he's obviously enjoying the party. Why don't you drill him on reincarnation and see if that'll help us out?"

"Okay, it'll only take about ten minutes."

After introducing myself, my opening salvo was, "I give lectures on reincarnation. Are you familiar with the concept?"

Twenty minutes later, the minister had more or less backed me into a corner while he tried to rescue me from what he considered, in so many words, New Age nonsense.

"With all due respect, sir," I said, "reincarnation is hardly new."

I started maneuvering us toward the open front door. After interrupting to thank him for coming, at least three times, I got us out to the sidewalk. Luckily, a family member took him off my hands. Back on the old-fashioned front porch, I checked over my shoulder to make sure he wasn't coming back. Half-a block away, in the direction he'd taken, I saw his tall elegant figure, in black, perched on a motorcycle, putt-putting down the tree-lined avenue.

A Former Catholic Priest

My Catholic neighbor and I had enjoyed debating spiritual issues for the last thirty years. One day, he suggested arranging a meeting between a former priest (and friend of his) and me. "He's a real scholar," said the neighbor, "so you'll have to be on your toes." The stated purpose was to debate spiritual issues, but I think the real reason was for him to witness his friend skewering my reincarnation arguments.

I was all for it. It would give me a golden opportunity to ask the questions about Catholicism I'd been saving for years but didn't want to ask my Catholic friends.

"You provide the Scotch and the house," said my neighbor, "and we'll be there, whatever evening you say."

They arrived on the appointed evening, and we settled in with Scotch all around. My neighbor looked like he was settling in for an enjoyable evening, and the priest and I were discreetly sizing each other up.

Four hours later, at midnight, we'd exhausted all discussions.

No bodies lay on the floor, much to my neighbor's disappointment. We'd reached détente. In response to my reincarnation Bible quotes in John 3, he'd refuted them with the party line. I hadn't rattled his cage and he hadn't budged my thinking. There was no enlightenment on either side.

Because he personally had informed me that he is a scholar, I asked him if he would consider reading a book or two on my reading list. Yes, he would. Would I do the same? Of course. At least, I'd had answers to my questions—some I could understand, some I couldn't.

Two weeks later, my neighbor informed me that his pal had enjoyed the discussion and wanted to know which book on my list, if he was going to read only one, I'd recommend.

Maybe I'm imagining another tiny victory.

This summer, six years after the evening, my neighbor mentioned that his friend would be delighted to have another meeting. I'm not sure I have the energy, but I appreciate his interest.

The Most Enlightened Minister Yet

Being invited to speak about reincarnation at the largest United Church in London was an honor. I've discussed the speech itself elsewhere in the book. But there's a story behind the invitation.

Apparently, when the subject of my speech reached the ears of the authority figures in the church, some of them took a dim view of it. But the young minister said, "Let's go for it—it'll make them think!"

The Quiet Believers

Every now and then, someone takes me aside and quietly admits that he or she has always felt reincarnation is a fact, and would like to know more about it. These are the old souls of the world, who have a knowing from so many past lives. Young souls need more structure in their religions. The more authoritarian the religion is, the younger the souls who embrace it.

Former Students

From time to time, I bump into someone from a *Study of Unseen Forces* classes I taught a few years ago. All of them mention how much the information on reincarnation meant to them. One of them said, "Now, when I sit and enjoy a sunset, I know where I fit in with the scheme of things, and I feel deliciously calm knowing I have future lives to live."

Stories from Friends and Acquaintances

From the variety of attitudes I've encountered over the years, I've learned the misconceptions people have about reincarnation. At least once a month, I hear someone say, "If I come back, I want to be a French poodle in a Jewish household," or "a cat, because a cat is God's way of showing that not everything in life has a purpose." Another standard is, "I've had enough trouble in this life, why would I ever want to come back?" From my Jewish friends I often hear, "Does that mean I can come back as a tree?" or "Are you crazy?" But there's one type of response that tests my sense of humor—and that's one that indicates contempt prior to investigation.

Pamela Evans

13
Summing Up

"The life which is not examined is not worth living."
—Plato

My first psychic reading started a quest that changed my life 180 degrees. It opened my eyes to a wider, more universal view of life, and started a feast of reading that continues to this day. The new knowledge has taught me where I fit in with the unseen forces around me—and why.

So few psychics and mediums are really good that, looking back over the last 20 years, I feel truly blessed to have met so many. And, because they've either lived in my hometown or visited, I haven't had to travel a long distance for a reading. The life-changing messages I've received from the best of them send a chill up my spine to this day.

Someone once described an analogy for the testimonies of people's experiences. "If you're sitting by the side of a road, and a thousand people pass you from left to right—each one saying, 'I've just crossed a bridge a mile back'— wouldn't you be inclined to believe there *is* a bridge a mile back?" So it is with the huge volume of clinical and scientific evidence for reincarnation.

I agree with the late Dr. Helen Wambach when she said, "I don't believe in reincarnation—I know it."

Without that first psychic reading from Mary—where I was thunderstruck by her information—I might never have had the interest in having my natal astrology chart drawn up. The information in my personal chart is priceless to me. It taught me who I am, and what I'm here to do, in this life.

The resulting understanding from seances, seminars, palmistry, books on soul ages and soul-mates, and stories from other people, have all added depth to my knowledge. I now know that Earth is a school and we're all in it together—though often in different classes.

The information in this book is not the result of a transcendental experience on my part. Anyone can experience similar enlightenment by reading and seeking out opportunities to gain insight from recommended psychics, mediums, astrologers, and so forth.

What I Know Now That I Didn't Know Then

- We must grow beyond the limited teachings of Christianity and Judaism, if these religions continue to refuse to reintroduce reincarnation to their teachings. Books with enlightened spiritual knowledge are listed on Web sites, at bookstores, or the library.

- Mark Twain said: "Loyalty to petrified opinion, never yet broke a chain or freed a human soul" (the inscription beneath his bust in the Hall of Fame).

- Things will go the way they're supposed to go.

- How we deal with life's obstacles is what matters, not whether or not we're successful.

Summing Up

We Grow Through Sorrow and Pain – Not Through Happiness

- Because we have many lifetimes and continue to learn in the spirit world, we never run out of time. Therefore, we can take our time and live life more fully in the present moment.

Reincarnation is a Compassionate System Because We Always Get Another Chance

- Our soul's major goals carry over from past lives. One of mine is fairness, which explains why I needed to know that life is ultimately fair (or else there was no purpose in living, as far as I was concerned).
- Hard work isn't always meant to produce success. In some cases, a soul is meant to struggle with little reward—perhaps to learn patience or perseverance. (Marge told me I was never meant to be as successful in the fashion business as I'd hoped, because I'm here to teach.)
- "Neither miscarriage nor abortion harms a soul. The soul often returns in the next pregnancy," says Dr. Brian Weiss in his latest book, *Messages from the Masters* (Warner Books).
- I must take responsibility for myself, and leave others free to choose what experiences they need for themselves.
- I am responsible for my own salvation. No one else can absolve me from wrong deeds.
- I chose my parents for the lessons they taught me in this life. I cannot blame them for my problems.
- Whatever is happening to me in this life is a result of choices I've made in the past.

- I now am aware of certain patterns in my life, and appreciate them for what they are.
- Bad things that happen to good people are chosen by their own souls, before they're born, for spiritual growth or to pay off a karmic debt.
- Mental illness results when the brain, which is like a radio, breaks down. Our mind is like the radio station: when a radio malfunctions, it doesn't mean that the radio station is not operative. Our minds never stop working—they are pure energy that can never be destroyed. My mother, who had Alzheimer's Disease, was able to communicate a special phrase she had always used when she was alive—through a medium—after she died.
- The death of a child is planned before birth by the child's soul which, with the advice of loving entities, agrees to come to Earth briefly to teach a lesson in grief. The child knows that he can soon return "home" again to the spirit world once his task is completed. The parents' sorrow usually starts a spiritual search for deeper understanding of the enigmas of life and death.
- Case histories show that sometimes the same soul returns later to the same family.
- Patience is one of the most important lessons we're here to learn. We need a physical body for such lessons that may come from a lingering illness, starvation, imprisonment, poverty, dealing with mental illness, family responsibilities, and so on. We can't learn patience in the spirit world, because everything there is instantaneous.
- The Golden Rule is the cardinal rule for living. It flows through every religion.
- Life does have justice, meaning, and purpose.

Summing Up

There Are Many Roads to Enlightenment

- As someone said, "If we're all going to end up sitting at the same table, does it matter what door we come through?"
- We never die, we merely change our level of consciousness.
- We always meet our loved ones again, sooner or later, in spirit and in body. Meeting a soul-mate is the ultimate evidence of this truth.
- We are divine beings. We have a divine origin and a divine destiny.
- I have said, "Ye are Gods; and all of you are children of the most high." (Psalm 82, Old Testament)
- Is it not written in your law, I said, "Ye are Gods." (Jesus, John 10:14, New Testament)
- Love is the strongest force in the universe.

In this book, I've explained, as simply as possible, some basic tools for self-knowledge. More comprehensive information is easily available. But, as with a computer, it isn't necessary to understand the complicated inner workings of the mechanism in order to use it effectively.

※ ※

No matter how many times we mess up our lives and fail to learn our lessons, we get another chance to get it right.

Twenty years ago, I was an agnostic—not sure that God existed. Now I'm not only certain that there is a God, but that he is a patient one. I'm also certain that I'll never be less conscious than I am at this moment—in other words, I'm as dead as I'll ever be.

※ ※

Pamela Evans

In conclusion, a poem by Colleen C. Hitchcock (*www.colleenhitchcock.com*):

ASCENSION

And if I go,
While you're still here...
Know that I live on,
Vibrating to a different measure
—behind a thin veil you cannot see through,
You will not see me.
So you must have faith
I wait till the time we can soar together again,
—both aware of each other,
Until then, live your life to its fullest.
And when you need me,
Just whisper my name in your heart,
...I will be there.

Appendix
Suggested Reading

Edgar Cayce

Cerminara, Gina. *Many Mansions* (Signet). The Edgar Cayce story on reincarnation.

Church, W.H. *Edgar Cayce's Story of the Soul* (ARE Press). Trace the fascinating footsteps of your evolving soul from its origin to its destiny.

Furst, Jeffery, ed. *Edgar Cayce's Story of Jesus* (Berkley Books).

Langley, Noel. *Edgar Cayce on Reincarnation* (Warner Books). Fully documented case histories of rebirth.

Stearn, Jess. *The Sleeping Prophet* (ARE Press). A biography of Edgar Cayce.

Evidence For Reincarnation

Bernstein, Morey. *The Search for Bridey Murphy* (Doubleday). The hypnotic regression case that created national interest in reincarnation.

Cranston, Sylvia and Carey Williams. *Reincarnation: A New Horizon in Science, Religion, and Society* (Theosophical University Press). Pulls together all aspects of the theory of reincarnation.

Fisher, Joe. *The Case for Reincarnation* (Grafton Press). Examines all the evidence for rebirth.

Moody, Raymond Jr. M.D. *Life After Life* (Bantam Books). The classic bestseller that offers astonishing proof of a life after physical death.

Perkins, James S. *Experiencing Reincarnation* (Quest). Everyone does remember past lives.

Shroder, Tom. *Old Souls* (Simon & Schuster). The scientific evidence for past lives.

Stevenson, Ian M.D. *20 Cases Suggestive of Reincarnation* (University of Virginia Press).

Stevenson, Ian M.D. *Where Reincarnation and Biology Intersect* (Praeger Publishing). Birthmarks match autopsy reports of children's former lives.

Wambach, Helen Ph.D. *Life Before Life* (Bantam Books). Case histories of astonishing journeys into past lives.

Wambach, Helen Ph.D. *Reliving Past Lives* (Barnes & Noble). The evidence in over 1,000 hypnosis-induced past-life recalls.

Whitton, Joel M.D. Ph.D., & Joe Fisher. *Life Between Life* (Dolphin Doubleday). Scientific explorations into the void separating one incarnation from the next.

Reincarnation in Religion

Cerminara, Gina. *Insights for the Age of Aquarius* (Quest). A handbook for religious sanity.

Gershom, Yonassan Rabbi. *Beyond the Ashes* (ARE Press). Cases of reincarnation from the Holocaust.

MacGregor, Geddes Ph.D. *Reincarnation As a Christian Hope* (Barnes & Noble).

MacGregor, Geddes Ph.D. *Reincarnation in Christianity* (Quest). A new vision of the role of rebirth in Christian thought.

Puryear, Henry Bruce. *Why Jesus Taught Reincarnation* (New Paradigm Press). A new key to understanding the scriptures.

True Experiences

Bowman, Carol. *Children's Past Lives* (Harper Collins). True cases of children's healing from knowledge of past lives.

Bowman, Carol. *Return from Heaven* (Harper Collins). Beloved relatives reincarnated within your family.

Cockell, Jenny. *Yesterday's Children* (Priatkus Books). Cockell's successful search for the "past-life family" which had haunted her from her earliest childhood.

Suggested Reading

Guirdham, Arthur. *The Cathars and Reincarnation* (C.W. Daniel Co. Ltd. England). A woman, through dreams and impressions in waking consciousness, remembers her life in the 13th century.

Stearn Jess. *The Search For the Girl With the Blue Eyes* (Bantam Books). The true story of a young woman's reincarnation.

Weiss, Brian M.D. *Many Lives, Many Masters* (Fireside Books, Simon and Schuster). A prominent psychiatrist, his young patient, and the past life therapy that changed both their lives.

Weiss, Brian M.D. *Only Love is Real* (Warner Books). Soul-mates reunited.

Astrology

Avery, Jeanne. *Astrology and Your Past Lives* (Fireside, Simon & Schuster). Explore past reincarnations through Saturn's placement in your chart.

Goodman, Linda. *Linda Goodman's Sun Signs* (Bantam Books). How to really know your husband, wife, lover, child, boss, employee, yourself, through astrology.

West, John Anthony. *The Case for Astrology* (ARKANA).

Odds and Ends

Bowen, Sandra, & F.R. Nocerino, Joshua Shapiro. *Mysteries of the Crystal Skulls Revealed* (J&S Aquarian Networking, Pacifica, CA).

de Saint-Germain, Comte C. *The Practice of Palmistry* (Newcastle Publishing Company Inc.).

Hunt, Stoker. *Ouija: The Most Dangerous Game* (Barnes & Noble). Investigates the history and legacy of the "Mystic Talking Oracle."

Stevens, Jose & Simon Warwick-Smith. *The Michael Handbook* (Warwick Press). "A Channeled System for Self Understanding."

Sutphen, Dick. *Unseen Influences* (Pocket Books, New York). A holistic approach to preventing attacks on your physical and mental health.

Tompkins, Peter & Christopher Bird. *The Secret Life of Plants* (Avon). A fascinating account of the physical, emotional, and spiritual relations between plants and man.

Vaughn, Alan. *Incredible Coincidence* (Signet).
Wilson, Ian. *In Search of Ghosts* (Macmillan). Tackles the key questions for which believers and skeptics demand answers.
Yarbro, Chelsea Quinn. *Messages From Michael* (Playboy Paperback). A serious search for the answers to age-old questions by a research team.

About the Author

Pamela Evans has spent the past 20 years researching reincarnation and the myriad theories and concept surrounding this controversial subject. She has read extensively, interviewed psychics, and tracked down people with real-life psychic experiences. She travels around North America lecturing on the subject, and is a popular guest on television and radio.

This book is a personal journey through her experiences that reaffirms that the knowledge of reincarnation brings hope, integrity, and meaning to our lives—and, most importantly, the understanding that life is fair.

Ms. Evans background also includes a stint as a commercial fashion illustrator and a fashion editor for a city magazine.

She lives with her husband David in London, Ontario, Canada, where they have raised two children.

The author can be reached at www.pamelajoyevans.com.

Products from Crossquarter Publishing Group

Crossquarter Breeze imprint: Integrating Body, Mind, Heart & Spirit

20 Herbs to Take on a Business Trip
Therese Francis, Ph.D.　　　　　ISBN: 1-890109-02-9
Herbal products to combat pre-presentation jitters, jetlag, diarrhea, insomnia, stiff muscles, and more.

20 Herbs to Take Outdoors: An Herbal First Aid Primer for the Outdoor Enthusiast
Therese Francis, Ph.D.　　　　　ISBN: 1-890109-02-9
Herbal products to combat pre-presentation jitters, jetlag, diarrhea, insomnia, stiff muscles, and more.

Attuning to the River of Kabbalah: Playing with Energy and Consciousness
Karen Kaufman Milstein, Ph.D.　　ISBN: 1-890109-38-X
Ancient Kabbalah meets modern energy psychology in the easy-to-use ASK technique.

Gods & Goddesses of the Zodiac: A Coloring Book by Anne Marie Garrison
Author: Anne Marie Garrison　　　ISBN: 1-890109-31-2
This delightful coloring book is a collection of Goddesses and Gods from around the world. A must for anyone interested in mythology or astrology.

Tellstones: Divination in a Welsh Tradition
Adam Bryn Tritt, Ph.D.　　　　　ISBN: 1-890109-32-0
Learn how to make and use the ancient, simple form of divination and magick called Tellstones.

The Mercury Retrograde Book: Surviving—Nay, Thriving—During Mercury Retrograde
Author: Therese Francis, Ph.D.　　ISBN: 1-890109-33-9
This book contains hundreds of ideas for you to do during the next Mercury retrograde interval that will improve, calm, and clarify your life.

Crossquarter Publishing Group Product Listing (continued)

Xemplar imprint: Autobiography and Visionary Fiction

My Heart and I (and Other Body Parts)
Jerry Danenberg   ISBN: 1-890109-36-3
One man's adventures in finding a cure for his heart disease.

Dead As I'll Ever Be
Pamela Evans   ISBN: 1-890109-37-1
One woman's travels through the psychic realms as she transforms from skeptic to believer.

Beyond One's Own: Healing Humanity in the Wake of Personal Tragedy
Gabriel Constans, PhD   ISBN: 1-890109-35-5
Gabriel Constans interviews 15 people who have transformed personal grief into social and political reform following a death in the family.

CrossTIME imprint: Science Fiction

Dark Days, Bright Futures I
                            ISBN: 1-890109-76-2
Fifteen short science fiction and urban fantasy stories from the 2001 CrossTIME Science Fiction contest.

Fenris Brothers imprint: Metaphysics

The Complete Concordance to Aleister Crowley's The Book of the Law (Liber AL vel Legis)
Compiled by Wolfgang Zeuner   ISBN: 1-890109-50-9
A meticulous listing of every word in the 1938 OTO edition of Liber Al, organized by book, paragraph number, and word number.

To Purchase Additional Titles

You can order additional copies of this book or other products from Crossquarter Publishing Group.

Mail to: **or fax to:**
Crossquarter Publishing Group   (505) 438-9846
PO Box 8756
Santa Fe, NM 87504-8756

Send me the following

Quantity	Product	Price (US$)
___	20 Herbs to Take Outdoors	$ 6.95
___	20 Herbs to Take on a Business Trip	$12.95
___	Attuning to the River of Kabbalah	$12.95
___	Beyond One's Own	$18.95
___	Concordance to The Book of the Law	$18.95
___	Dark Days, Bright Futures I	$12.95
___	Dead As I'll Ever Be	$15.95
___	Gods & Goddesses of the Zodiac	$ 6.95
___	My Heart & I	$15.95
___	Tellstones	$12.95
___	The Mercury Retrograde Book	$12.95

Shipping ($1/item) _____
SUBTOTAL _____
6.5% Sales Tax for New Mexico addressess _____
TOTAL _____

Name _____
Address _____
City _____ State ___ Zip _____
Phone Number (in case of questions) (___) _____

How are you paying (please check one):
__ Check or money order made to Crossquarter
__ Credit card __ Visa __ Mastercard __ AmX

Account Number _____
Expiration Date _____
Signature _____

Please allow 4-6 weeks for delivery.